THE GOSPEL
IN SLOW MOTION

THE GOSPEL
IN SLOW MOTION

RONALD KNOX

CLUNY
Providence, Rhode Island

CLUNY MEDIA EDITION, 2022

For more information regarding this title
or any other Cluny Media publication,
please write to info@clunymedia.com, or to
Cluny Media, P.O. Box 1664, Providence, RI 02901

VISIT US ONLINE AT WWW.CLUNYMEDIA.COM

The Gospel in Slow Motion copyright © Lady Magdalen Howard 1950

Published by permission.

Cluny Media edition copyright © 2022 Cluny Media LLC

ISBN (PAPERBACK): 978-1685950842
ISBN (HARDCOVER): 978-1685952181

ALL RIGHTS RESERVED

NIHIL OBSTAT: Georgius D. Smith, S. Th.D., *Censor Deputatus*

IMPRIMATUR: Edm. Can. Surmont, *Vic. Gen.*
WESTMONASTERII, DIE 27 JULII 1950

Cover design by Clarke & Clarke
Cover image: Francisco de Zurbarán, *Saint Matthew*,
1637/1639, oil on canvas
Courtesy of Museo de Cádiz

CONTENTS

PREFACE		i
CHAPTER 1.	Alive to God	1
CHAPTER 2.	By Candle-Light	11
CHAPTER 3.	The Playmate	19
CHAPTER 4.	The Boast of an Apostle	27
CHAPTER 5.	How to Assert Ourselves	37
CHAPTER 6.	A Saint of Last Century	45
CHAPTER 7.	The Weed Killer	55
CHAPTER 8.	St. Peter Looks Back	63
CHAPTER 9.	The Devil Goes House-Hunting	73
CHAPTER 10.	The Test	83
CHAPTER 11.	The Magi and the Centurion	91
CHAPTER 12.	Seed-Time	101
CHAPTER 13.	A Caution	109
CHAPTER 14.	The No-Men	117
CHAPTER 15.	Resolutions	125
CHAPTER 16.	God's Good Marks	133
CHAPTER 17.	An Old Favourite	141
CHAPTER 18.	The Apostle of the Midlands	153
CHAPTER 19.	An Uncomfortable Saint	161
CHAPTER 20.	The Lump	169
CHAPTER 21.	Ups and Downs	179
CHAPTER 22.	Man the Misfit	187
CHAPTER 23.	The Report	195

To Gerry Ann

PREFACE

SERMON-TIME MAKES EXACTING CLAIMS ON THE PARISH priest. Year after year, Sunday after Sunday, he watches, from his pulpit, the same congregation settle down into its attitude of defensive repose. And how is he to avoid monotony? About today's Gospel, today's feast, they have heard what he has to say already. I have never been a parish priest; but during the war years I found myself in the position of involuntary chaplain to a convent school, and I was faced by the same difficulty. I fell back, like better men before me, on the expedient of giving courses of pulpit instruction. One of these was published afterwards under the title of *The Mass in Slow Motion*; another as *The Creed in Slow Motion*; and, from the kind letters people sent, I gathered that they had an appeal for others besides school-girls. Couldn't I do another (I was asked) about this and that? And I was forced to admit, sadly, that it wasn't possible without my congregation, that admirable, that eager congregation. There were no more courses for publication; I had shot my bolt.

Yet there were occasions on which I had addressed myself, like any other parish priest, to the day's gospel or epistle, to the day's

RONALD KNOX

Saint, taking no thought for the morrow, not troubling to work them up into a series. A good number of these occasional sermons had silted up in my archives, and it was suggested to me that some of these might make up, albeit rather raggedly, into a volume. My title, *The Gospel in Slow Motion*, is not altogether easy to justify; no attempt has been made to follow the outlines of the gospel story. But I like to think that they are, for the most part, "Gospel" sermons; by which I mean that they aimed at producing good Christians rather than *dévotes*. And if St. Paul is only the Gospel at second-hand, the hand was an uncommonly sure instrument.

I have nothing to add by way of introduction, except that (as before) I have not pruned the original typescript a great deal. Illustrations and allusions which may seem, to the casual reader, frivolous or obscure, must nevertheless be pardoned; pardoned for the sake of a few special readers, who remember Aldenham, and the farm, and the Shore Pool, and above all the Chapel.

R. A. KNOX
Mells, 1950

THE GOSPEL
IN SLOW MOTION

CHAPTER I

Alive to God

So he took ship across the sea, and came to his own city. And now they brought before him a man who was palsied and bed-ridden; whereupon Jesus, seeing their faith, said to the palsied man, Son, take courage, thy sins are forgiven. And at this, some of the scribes said to themselves, He is talking blasphemously. Jesus read their minds, and said, Why do you cherish wicked thoughts in your hearts? Tell me, which command is more lightly given, to say to a man, Thy sins are forgiven, or to say, Rise up, and walk? And now, to convince you that the Son of Man has authority to forgive sins while he is on earth (here he spoke to the palsied man), Rise up, take thy bed with thee, and go home. And he rose up, and went back to his house, so that the multitudes were filled with awe at seeing it, and praised God for giving such powers to men. (MATT. 9:1–8)

THAT GOSPEL WANTS EXPLAINING AT ONE OR TWO POINTS, doesn't it? It is about a palsied man—that is, a paralysed man—who was brought to our Lord to be healed. I say, he was *brought*, because, being paralysed, he couldn't come himself; he had to be carted about by his friends, bed and all. And our Lord consented to cure him, we are told, because he "saw their faith"; how does that

RONALD KNOX

work out, exactly? Because after all there were crowds of sick people queueing up to get healed wherever our Lord went, and a lot of them must have been stretcher cases; what was there about this one party which showed that they had got faith, even if the others hadn't? Sometimes in the gospels you can't find the answer to a question like that, but here you can; because St. Mark and St. Luke, who have accounts of the same incident, have both remembered to put in something which St. Matthew forgot to put in—in fact, you may almost say that St. Matthew left out the point of the story. The paralysed man was being carried, in his bed, by four friends; and when they got to Capharnaum, they found that our Lord was preaching inside a house; the house was quite full, and there was a crowd round the doors, and the whole place looked rather like Paddington Station in the holiday season. One thing was quite clear: there wasn't going to be room to carry a bed with a sick man on it through all that mess; no amount of "By your leave" was going to make those people shift.

So what did the four friends do? They climbed up on to the roof, and lugged the sick man up after them. Then they made a big hole in the roof by taking the tiles away and let the bed down through it. That seems a rather fishy part of the story, doesn't it? Probably some of you have watched a house being built, in the days when it was still possible to get houses built; or you may have been up into the attics (which are almost as good fun as the cellars) and looked up at the odd sloping ceiling that attics have. If so, you will know that tiles don't float about in the air; they have wooden rafters to rest on. So, you very rightly ask, how on earth did the bed get through the rafters? The answer to that one (which I had

The Gospel in Slow Motion

to look up in a book) is that in Palestine, where things are different from England, and a roof is more meant to keep the sun off than keep the rain off, the tiles used to rest on flat hurdles of wickerwork, each of them rather like the top of a very large clothes-basket; and you could take away a length or two of that stuff, tiles and all, before the owner of the house could get up on to the roof and say, "Here, what's the great idea?" So that part's all right; they took away a hurdle or two, with the tiles, and let down the bed just in front of where our Lord was preaching. It sounds rather apt to give the people inside distractions; but I expect when our Lord was preaching you didn't watch the back hair of the girl in front of you, you stood still and listened.

Then there's one other puzzle which I think my translation makes rather less of a puzzle than the old one did. The old translation was, "Whether is it easier to say, Thy sins be forgiven thee, or to say, Arise and walk?" To which one is inclined to answer that there's not much in it. I think it does become a little clearer if you translate it, "Which command is more lightly given?" The point is, not whether you can *say* these things, but whether you can get away with it. Our Lord has told the sick man, "Thy sins are forgiven thee"; and that, he points out, is a perfectly safe thing to say, because nobody can know whether it's true or not. But if you say to a person "Rise up and walk," and he doesn't do anything of the kind, it gives you away; everybody can see that you haven't any powers of healing after all. So we'll try saying *that*, our Lord tells them, and then you'll be able to see for yourselves whether my word goes or not.... You there, on the bed, rise, and take up your bed and go back home on your two feet. And of course the man did.

RONALD KNOX

Don't let's make an extra difficulty about how the man carried his bed; it wasn't one of those great iron beds that are such an awful nuisance to shift, even when they're on wheels. It was just a sort of mattress which you could roll up and carry on your back. No, the question I want to put to you, which you probably hadn't thought of putting to yourself, is this: Who was it that our Lord was ordering about when he said, Rise up? What was the good of telling the man to rise up if he was paralysed? You might as well tell him to fly. Of course if he had been shamming, it would have been different; I dare say you've been told to get out of bed before now when you didn't want to. But he wasn't shamming, he was paralysed; that is to say, his nervous system wasn't working. Your nervous system is like a lot of telegraph wires, as it were, which send out messages from your will to your muscles and make your body do what you want it to do. Somebody told me that one uses five hundred different muscles in getting up out of an armchair; so when you decide to get up out of an armchair your will has to send five hundred different telegrams, as it were; which is perhaps why the performance doesn't always go with quite such a bang as you'd expect. If you're paralysed, the whole of that telegraph system is out of order; you get "Sorry, no reply" every time. So what was the good of telling the man to get out of bed? He'd been trying to for years, but he couldn't bring it off.

What I want you to see is that although our Lord addressed his remark to the man himself, he was really issuing his orders not to the man himself, not to his will, but to those nerves of his which to all appearance had been dead these years past. Only they weren't dead really; our Lord was God, and to God all things are

The Gospel in Slow Motion

alive. That is how we start Matins of the Dead, by repeating, "To God, all things are alive; come, let us adore him." The waves on the sea of Galilee, threatening the tiny boat on which the apostles were rowing, were lifeless things as far as the apostles were concerned; you couldn't get the sea to keep quiet by throwing them a biscuit, as if it had been an angry dog. But to our Lord, who was God, they were alive; he just gets up and talks to them with the quiet, stand-no-nonsense voice of a schoolmaster controlling his class when they are being rowdy, and they all grow calm at once. So it was when he came across the fig tree that was all leaves and didn't bear any fruit; as a sign to his disciples, to show them what a dangerous thing false piety was, he said to the fig tree, "Let no man ever eat fruit of thee henceforward," and it withered up the same day. The whole of nature, if I may use a very undignified expression, "sat up and took notice" when our Lord passed by. Richard Crashaw, one of the greatest of our English Catholic poets, went in as an undergraduate at Cambridge for a Latin poetry prize; and the subject he was told to write on was the miracle at Cana of Galilee. And at the end of the three hours he showed up one line, which means, "The shame-faced water saw its Lord, and blushed." He got the prize. To the poet's view, the well-water at Cana reacted, when our Lord confronted it, exactly as you would react if you went out to tea somewhere and suddenly found yourself being introduced to the Queen; it blushed. Once, in curing a sick person, our Lord did actually address, not the sick person, but the disease. He found St. Peter's mother-in-law lying sick of a fever, and he didn't say to her, Get well. He rebuked the fever, and it left her. The germs obeyed him.

RONALD KNOX

Everything in nature behaved as if it were alive when our Lord spoke, except one thing—human wills like yours and mine. "Jerusalem, Jerusalem, how often have I been ready to gather thy children, as a hen gathers her chickens under her wings, and thou didst refuse it!" He tried so hard to get the Jews to believe in him, and they pretended not to see. "Have I not chosen all twelve of you, and one of you is a devil?" He tried so hard to make Judas repent in time, but Judas behaved as if his heart was dead. And, after all, that is what is going on the whole time. Almighty God reigns in heaven, issuing his orders to a dumb universe, which obeys; issuing his orders to living souls, yours and mine, and we don't listen; we sham dead. Even where we ourselves are concerned, he controls all the unconscious movements of our bodies. If you've got pins and needles as you sit there, it means your body is obeying God's will. If you yawn as you sit there, it may be that your mind is not attending to me very much, but your body is attending all right, attending to God. That yawn came because he told it to. You can go further than that, and say that the unconscious part of your mind is always alive to God's will. You know how you find yourself suddenly humming a tune, and say to yourself, "Good gracious, I wonder what on earth put that tune into my head? I can't have heard it played for years." No, you didn't recall it to memory by any conscious act of your will. It dug itself up, somehow, from the lumber-room of useless old memories that is called your unconscious mind; and it dug itself up because God told it to. It's only when his call comes to your conscious mind, to your will, that it is sometimes disobeyed. Aren't we miserable sort of creatures? God's favourite creatures, his spoilt children; we alone, in a listening universe, say "No" to him.

The Gospel in Slow Motion

That is why the spiritual writers, when they want to put us in our place, tell us that we ought to try and serve God as well as his dumb creatures do. For instance, his dumb creatures obey his commands at once, without stopping to ask questions. When somebody fires off a gun a few yards away, it's a sort of race between the flash and the report, to see whether the flash can reach your eyes or the report reach your ears first. When you throw a hairbrush out of the window, its speed increases as it gets nearer the ground, like the creatures in *Alice in Wonderland* saying "Faster, faster!" because the law of gravitation tells it to. When the inside of your nose tickles, the sneeze (which is a reaction of your body) comes bursting out as if there were not a moment to be lost. And now think of you, when you're told to do something. You hang about saying, "Oh, but Mother!" just to waste time; you know that you'll have to do the thing sooner or later. You know God wants you to do what the nuns tell you to, but you can't do it at once; you *must* hop round on one leg and put in a lot of this "Oh, but Mother!" business before you get the thing done. Try to be more like a hairbrush thrown out of a window; try to be a bit more of a sneeze.

And then there's another thing: the dumb creatures obey God's will steadily, patiently, going through the same performance hour after hour, day after day, without complaining that they are getting tired of it. The damson trees in the orchard don't suddenly say to themselves, one autumn, "Look here, I'm tired of these everlasting damsons; let's make it horse-chestnuts this year!" The Shore Pool doesn't suddenly say, "How boring it is always staying put in this muddy hole! I'm going up to the front drive to see a bit of life!" No, the Shore Pool stays at its post, where God put it, and the damson trees go on churning out damsons, because that was what God told them to do. It's *we* who are always making such a fuss and bother about having to do the same old things; same old French, same old Latin—as though it would cheer us up no end if Latin were quite a different language tomorrow from what it was yesterday. We are got down, aren't we, merely by the fact that bedtime is the same every day, and meal-times are the same every day, quite irrespective of whether the bedtime is too early, or the meal-times too late. And the spiritual writers say, "Look at you! Why can't you be more like the Shore Pool?"

They spare us nothing, do they? Because, having scolded us for our impatience in that way, the next thing they point out is that the dumb creatures are prepared to obey God's will even when it means going contrary to their own natures. That happened, you see, every time our Lord did a miracle. When he walked on the water, the water had to behave as if it were dry ground. And we, they point out, aren't at all like that; if God asks anything of us which seems to be beyond our powers we make a great fuss and bother about it, like the cook when she says it isn't her place to bath the baby. Really, we say, that is asking too much of a person like me! As if the paralysed man had said, "Yes, but, Lord, this bed is frightfully heavy!" We ought to be ready for *any* demand God makes of us, even if he calls upon us for heroic effort, heroic self-denial; he will give us grace, after all, to see the things through.

The spiritual writers are rather depressing sort of people, aren't they? At the beginning of a new term especially. Well, don't let's be depressed about it and get all mopey about the miserable creatures we are. Nothing so paralyses us as thinking we are paralysed. Let's just keep those three words at the back of our minds all the time, alive to god. Please let me know clearly, Lord, as soon as you want me to do something for you; and then let's try if we can't do it.

CHAPTER 2

By Candle-Light

*And it shall come to pass at that time that
I will search Jerusalem with candles.* (ZEPH. 1:12)

CANDLEMAS DAY IS RATHER AN OBSCURE FEAST; OBSCURE, I mean, in its origins. If you will look up in the *Encyclopaedia Britannica* the name of that old pagan festival which was called the Lupercalia, you will find it stated that in A.D. 494 this festival was "changed into the feast of the Purification." That's the sort of statement that always enchants me, because it's so typical of all the bogus stuff that is written nowadays about the history of religion. At the Lupercalia a band of young men sacrificed a goat and a dog, smeared the blood on their foreheads, and then ran round the city hitting everybody they met with leather thongs. So in A.D. 494 Pope Gelasius thought there wasn't much point in that, and "changed it" into the feast of Candlemas. You can imagine the old-fashioned people in Rome saying, "Of course, it's not quite the same as the old thing, but it's the same sort of thing, anyhow." When you've digested that nonsense, you look up the article on Candlemas, in the same edition of the *Encyclopaedia Britannica*. And you find that the feast of Candlemas originated in the East long before it came to Rome, and that the Candlemas procession only began at Rome in the year 687, practically two hundred years after the Lupercalia were abolished. And the lesson of that, which is a very important lesson, is that you shouldn't believe one half of the things you see in print; probably not more than one quarter of the things you see in print. Because they aren't true.

Well, when you've cut out all the learned stuff, the reason why we celebrate our Lady's Purification on 2nd February is clear enough. It is just forty days after Christmas, or rather, it is the fortieth day after Christmas, if you put both it and Christmas Day into the sum. That, as you probably know, was the rather confusing way in which the ancients used to reckon. I've worked it all out very carefully, so don't bother to do it in your head instead of listening to what I'm saying. Forty days after the birth of her child, a Jewish woman was expected to go up to the temple and give thanks to God. And at the same time she *redeemed* the child which had been born to her; the child, in theory, belonged to God, and she had to buy it back from God by offering him the sacrifice of a lamb. Only if you were very poor, as our Lady and St. Joseph were very poor, you could sacrifice a pair of turtle-doves or two young pigeons instead. That is the event, then, which we celebrate today. Why it is the custom to bless candles and carry them round in procession isn't so clear. But whatever gave rise to the custom, it is obviously appropriate to the occasion, because it was on this occasion, if you remember, that an old prophet called Simeon greeted the child Jesus with the hymn we call the *Nunc dimittis*, which is sung every night at Compline. And at the end of that hymn he says that our

The Gospel in Slow Motion

Lord will be "the light which shall give revelation to the Gentiles, the glory of thy people Israel." The candle, in Christian ceremonies, is always meant to remind us of Christ, who is the light of the world. That is why the sponsor has to hold a candle when a child is baptized; that is why the Paschal candle is blessed and lit and dipped into the font on Easter Eve. He is the Light which lightens every man coming into the world; and the Church, remembering old Simeon's prophecy, tries to give expression to this idea of Light shining in darkness by making a great display of candle-light; that is really all you can say about it.

Only I thought, this afternoon, I would try to give a new twist to the same idea. We didn't have a candle-procession here this morning, because there is so little room for processions in this chapel, and we should have burnt one another's hair a good deal if we had tried. But many of you have been in church, before now, on Candlemas Day or on some other occasion when each member of the congregation had a lighted candle to carry. Have you ever noticed, in the course of your distractions on such an occasion, how different a person's face looks when it has a candle held quite close to it? You get unaccustomed shadows and highlights on it, the eyebrows show up more, and altogether it's quite a different face. The effect varies; sometimes you find that a friend is much better-looking under that treatment, sometimes that she is much plainer. We don't all of us light up equally well. And when the prophet Zephaniah represents Almighty God as saying, "I will search Jerusalem with candles," that is the sort of picture it conveys to my mind. Probably they would be portable oil-lamps, really, but the effect would be the same. I think of the face of everyone in Jerusalem suddenly lit up by having a candle held close to it, looking somehow quite different. And then I try to think what it would be like if everybody, instead of having their faces suddenly lit up like that, could have their consciences suddenly lit up like that. And then I reflect that that is what did happen in Jerusalem, what did happen in the world, when Christ, the great Light, the great Lamp of Truth, came into it. Everyone who came close to him showed up in a new way in that light; everyone's conscience was thrown into strong relief, as people's features are thrown into strong relief by candle-light, and you saw the dark lines drawn darker; and people who had hitherto been quite obscure suddenly appeared in shining beauty of the soul, while others who had seemed only moderately evil till then suddenly showed up as hideous, almost monstrous to look at. That was what happened when the Light came into the world, and those who were his own did not receive him. He divided the world, wherever he went, into two classes: the people who loved him, and the people who hated him; the people who shouted "Hosanna," and the people who shouted "Crucify him."

If you remember the story in the gospel, you will remember that Simeon had some more to say, when he met the child Jesus in the temple, besides the *Nunc dimittis*. He said, "This child is destined to bring about the fall of many and the rise of many in Israel"; the rise or the fall—you rose or you fell when you met him; you did not stay where you were. Peter met him, and rose from being a plain fisherman to being the prince of the apostles. Judas met him, and fell from being his trusted companion to being the traitor who handed him over. The rise and fall of many in Israel, and for a sign which shall be spoken against; he comes to the world as a sign that

The Gospel in Slow Motion

God is at last having mercy on his people, visiting them to redeem them from their sins. But that sign will only get its message across to a few; there will be others, alas, there will be many others, who will speak against that sign, turn their backs on it and pretend not to notice it. And then Simeon goes on, "That the thoughts of many hearts may be revealed." The thoughts were there all the time, but they were not revealed; people did not make their inner thoughts fully known, even to themselves, until our Lord came, the Candle that threw its light into the recesses of their consciences and showed them up for what they were. The shepherds on the hill were good honest shepherd folk, that was all; they went and saw the child Jesus in his crib, and it turned them into Christian missionaries. Herod was a wicked man, everybody knew that; but nobody knew how abominably cruel he was until a child was born in Bethlehem, and he sent round and massacred the Holy Innocents—Christmas Day showed him up for the treacherous coward he was. Everybody who came across Jesus of Nazareth was either the better or the worse for it.

So it was all through his life. So it was here, in the temple; Simeon, specially warned by the Holy Spirit to go into the temple just when he did, takes the child in his arms; and as the child smiles up at him, that smile lights up his old face as if with candle-light, and he becomes a prophet. So it is with Anna, the widow who is mentioned just afterwards; she merely catches sight of the child, it would seem, and is so moved by the encounter that she goes about speaking of it to all those who were in Jerusalem. And all through his life our Lord has this strange power of compelling the allegiance of all the people who have their hearts in the right place;

the thoughts of those hearts are revealed, they come and tell him about their troubles, they confess their sins to him, they ask to become his disciples. Mary Magdalen, guilty though she has been, falls at his feet in floods of tears; meanwhile Simon the Pharisee, who is our Lord's host on that occasion, can do no more than reveal to the world, echoing down posterity, the accents of his miserable pride. The Pharisees as a whole show up badly, don't they, in that divine candle-light? All his kindness, all his patience, all his works of mercy, only make them hate our Lord the more. And so at the last they hurry him to a cross; and even on the Cross he divides the world into those who love him and those who hate him; the thief on one side of him turns his face towards the light, and it is irradiated with the promise of a happy eternity; the thief on the other side turns his face away, and goes out into the darkness to which he belongs. Wherever he goes, our Lord reveals men's hearts, and we see them either lit up by his presence, or shown up in all the dark lineaments of their pride, their hatred, and their guilt.

But there was one person, after all, whom this heavenly candle-flame illuminated more than any other, flooded with light. We haven't quite finished yet with the things Simeon said. When he told our Lady that the effect of her Son's appearance in Israel would be to reveal the thoughts of many hearts, he gave her this additional piece of information: "Thy own soul a sword shall pierce." Other people's hearts will unfold their goodwill, or their wickedness, to a more or less degree, as they come in contact, to a more or less degree, with this little Son of yours. But you, who have been closer to him, who will always be closer to him than any other, *your* heart will be torn open as with a sword for all the world to see the treasures it contains. That prophecy, as we know, was verified on Calvary. When we contemplate our Lady in the stable, by the crib, the beauty of her is blinding enough, as she is lit up by the rays of the Child she holds in her arms. The humility which he showed in coming to earth is reflected in the humility with which she adapts herself to those wretched surroundings, the dark cave, and the manger, and the cold. The kindness of God our Saviour which appeared, St. Peter tells us, in his coming down to redeem us from our sins, is reflected in that love which lights up her features; all that love drawn from him and given back to him. But we have not yet really seen the Heart of Mary. The Heart of Mary is not torn open, exposed fully to our view, until we see her standing beside the Cross; the great fire of charity which burned in the Heart of the Crucified playing on her features as she stands there, and lighting them up with a glow as red as the glow of martyrdom. We have not really seen the Heart of Mary until we learn to recognize the amazing considerateness with which she allowed him, all his life, to take his own course, though she knew where that course would lead, never asking him to hold back from the thought of what it would mean to her; until we learn to guess something of the compassionate love with which she grieved over the outrages done to him; grieved, in doing so, over our sins, and offered her satisfaction for them in union with his. That sword of sorrow opens to us the Heart of our Lady, as the centurion's lance opened for us the Heart of our Lord.

Well, I haven't time to say much more; I would only remind you, by way of conclusion, that we too, after all these centuries, rise or fall according as we accept or reject this Sign, so much spoken against, who is the Saviour and the judge of the world. We who are brought so close to our Lord in the Holy Eucharist, will not our consciences show up, the brighter or the darker, the more beautiful or the more deformed, for the brightness with which the rays of that presence shine upon us? How much more glaring in a Christian, in a Catholic, in a frequent communicant, are those blemishes of character which we hardly notice in some friend who has escaped the influence of religion altogether! The selfishness, the uncharity, the meanness, the self-indulgence, the half-heartedness of so many Christians, how cruelly they show up in the Light that streams from Christ crucified! Like master, like man, says the proverb; and we, who know only one Master, Christ, how is it that there is such a discrepancy between his life and ours, between his way of looking at things and ours? Let us ask our Blessed Lady, on this joyful and sorrowful feast of her Purification, to teach us something of the secret by which her Heart, at Bethlehem and on Calvary, became the mirror and the counterpart of her Son's; let us ask him to show us our own consciences, under the illumination of his dazzling purity, teaching us how to be sorry for our sins, and making our hearts, our cold, detached hearts, share something of the burning charity which kindled his.

CHAPTER 3

The Playmate

*Making play before him, with the whole world
for my playground.* (Prov. 8:30–31)

THE BOOK OF PROVERBS ISN'T QUITE EVERYBODY'S MONEY. For the most part it is a set of short comments on life and human nature written nearly three thousand years ago; and it is hardly to be wondered at that a good many of those things should have been said more than once since then, and should have lost something of the thrill of novelty. We still use some of them: "Spare the rod and spoil the child," for example, is a proverb of King Solomon's, though one cynical person did point out that, when he said it, King Solomon was very much in the position of the headmaster of a large public school. Every now and then you light on something which is rather pleasant in the Proverbs; I think my favourite verse is: "He that blesses his neighbour, rising up early in the morning and blessing him, the same shall be a curse unto him"; I used sometimes to feel like that when people came and woke me up with *Benedicamus Domino* at the Seminary. But on the whole it is the spirit of the book, I think, rather than the detail of it, that Almighty God wants us to learn something from. And the spirit of the book may be summed up in two words, get wisdom. By wisdom, it doesn't mean knowing all the dates of the kings of England, or all the capitals of the South American republics—although of course those are very useful things to know. It means learning to see things straight, and to see which things are worthwhile and which aren't. And since it is taken for granted that the readers of the book are people who believe in Almighty God, it goes without saying that no wisdom is any use which doesn't take into account the fact that God exists, and that he has given man commandments, and that man has duties towards him.

And there is one famous passage in which Wisdom is personified, and makes a long speech asserting her own claim to the loyalty of the human heart. It begins, "The Lord possessed me [that is, possessed Wisdom] before his creation began," Mind was there, Intellect was there, from the first go. We, brought up on the leavings of nineteenth-century science, are apt to think as if it was the other way round. We think of the world in which we live starting as a lot of slime all covered with mist, and then gradually producing vegetation, grass and bracken and so on, and then fish and then birds and then animals and so gradually working up to Man, and with Man you get Mind. Well, it's all true as far as it goes—in fact it's very much what the book of Genesis tells us; but it is nonsense to suppose that Mind came in as a kind of afterthought at the end. How could you have an afterthought without a Mind already there to think it? So the point of this whole passage is that Mind was there from the start, God's Mind, God's Wisdom. Human wisdom, the wisdom you and I laboriously acquire by looking out of the window while we are being told about the South American republics, is only a reflection, a participation, of that Divine Wisdom which exists in God. He never had to acquire it; he possessed it from the first; it was part of his infinite perfection, inseparable from his own nature.

Well, let me just read you the whole passage, now that you know what it is about. "The Lord was master of me when first he went about his work, at the birth of time, before his creation began. Long, long ago, before earth was fashioned, I held my course. I lay in the womb already, when the depths were not yet in being, when no springs of water had yet broken. When I was born, the mountains had not yet sunk on their firm foundation, and there were no hills; not yet had he made the dry land or the rivers or the solid framework of the world. I was there when he spread out the heavens, when he fenced in the waters with a vault inviolable, when he fixed the sky overhead, and gave rest to the fountain-springs of the deep. I was there when he enclosed the sea within its confines, forbidding the waters to transgress their assigned limits, when he poised the foundations of the earth. I was at his side, a master-workman, my delight growing from one day to the next, as I made play before him all the while, with the whole world for my playground. And now I take delight in the company of Adam's children. Listen to me, then, you that are my sons, that follow, to your happiness, in the paths I show you; listen to the learning that will make you wise, instead of turning away from it. Blessed are they that listen to me, keeping watch, day after day, at my threshold, and waiting for my doors to open. The man who wins me, wins life; drinks deep of the Lord's favour."

RONALD KNOX

I don't think that needs much more explanation. Three things about the world of nature seem to have impressed the Jewish mind particularly. One was the mountains, naturally, because Palestine is a very mountainous country; the slopes of it are so steep and sudden that you thought of them as having been piled up by Almighty God, like the sand-castles you and I used to make on the beach when we were small. And the sea, always keeping its own limits, and not encroaching on the dry land; that was a permanent source of wonder to the Jews, because they had two inland seas in their own country, as we know, the Dead Sea and the Sea of Galilee, both of them well below sea level, which sounds odd. If you dug a canal through the middle of Palestine the waters of the Mediterranean would come flooding down into those two great lakes. So the Jews thought of Almighty God as conducting the sea about in channels, very much as you and I did when we made a moat round the sand-castle and persuaded the sea to flow into it. And the third thing which impressed them was the springs, coming bubbling up out of nowhere. Very important to the Jews, because the rivers out there all run dry or nearly dry in the summer-time, and you want wells all over the place to keep the cattle alive. So these mysterious holes in the earth which God seemed to have dug right down into the waters under the earth, were a matter of special interest to the Jews. Just so, if you remember, if you dug a hole in the sand with your father's umbrella, the water used to come bubbling up of its own accord. Hills and the sea and the springs, those were the exciting facts of creation. And the Hebrew poet thought of Wisdom, of Mind, as God's playmate when he first took to playing sand-castles in this rich world of our experience; much as your mother sat beside you, and helped you to make sand-castles on the beach. "My delight growing from one day to the next I believe, though I can't prove, that that refers to the seven days of creation; the whole thing working up to its grand climax in man. Since then, Wisdom has delighted in the company of Adam's children; the Divine Wisdom is mysteriously somehow reflected and repeated, inside here. And therefore, says Wisdom, it is a good thing for you men to queue up at my doors first thing in the morning, like the Bridgnorth people at the fishmonger's.

One question you are all burning to ask, and very sensibly: Why does the Church want us to think about all this when we are celebrating a feast of our Blessed Lady? I haven't time to go into all that; and it would be rather dull because I should have to discuss the meanings of Hebrew verbs, and the heresies of the fourth century. We had quite enough last Sunday about the heresies of the fourth century, and how the Church had to swerve and duck to avoid them. So you will have to take it from me that the Church thought it would be rather jolly to apply all this to our Lady. And you see, when you come to think of it, the whole point of our Lady is that she comes in just when God decides to remake the world. That first creation, in which the Hebrew poet saw the Divine Wisdom as God's accomplice, working out the whole design and going through the plans with him, was all spoilt by the Fall of Man. Everything was at sixes and sevens because Man, the ruler of this planet, had got his nature twisted all out of shape, and in a sense the whole process had to be begun again, like mending a broken toy. In that process of mending the world, once more God had an accomplice. But in this case it wasn't just something of himself, his Wisdom, poetically considered as being there on the spot to help. It was a real woman of flesh and blood, really there on the spot to help. It was our Lady accepting the message of Gabriel that, humanly speaking, made the Incarnation possible.

God became Man, to remake his world; he became a little child, and I suppose he used to play games; I don't think the Sacred Humanity would have been quite human if our Lord had never played games. And the best playmate he had, if so, was his Blessed Mother, such a short distance away from girlhood herself, who was so good at sympathizing, at seeing other people's points of view. At any rate, she was the Wisdom which accompanied him through all those steps of early childhood. Our Lord had, if he cared to use it, all the knowledge which is enjoyed by the blessed Saints in heaven. But, in order to be perfectly Man, he preferred to acquire knowledge by experience and by hearsay, just as you and I do. He went to school in the carpenter's shop; but his education had begun long before that. He had been learning all the time, "increasing in wisdom," the gospel tells us. And the person who taught him that wisdom was his mother—who else should it be?

So when you get this bit of Proverbs used instead of an epistle on feasts of our Lady, you aren't expected to think of her as present at the Creation and helping Almighty God to make the mountains; she wasn't. It's a good thing to remember sometimes that there is a limit to the compliments you can pay to our Blessed Lady. I remember when we were revising the Westminster Hymnal we had to consider one day in committee a hymn by Father Faber, addressed to her. And a friend of mine, who is a very good theologian, said, "The second verse of this hymn begins with the question, And art

The Gospel in Slow Motion

thou really infinite? The answer to that is, No." So we didn't put that hymn in. No, you haven't got to think of our Lady as God's wise playmate when he made the world. Enough to remember that she was the wise playmate of God Incarnate, when he re-made the world.

You have to think of a mother and her little son, who is just learning to talk in words of one syllable. They are looking out, from some point a bit west of Nazareth, at the great mass of Mount Carmel dominating the plain. And the boy asks, "Ma zeh?" (What's that?). And his mother answers, "That's ha-har [the mountain]; say 'Har,' Jesus." Or they are a bit east of Nazareth, and suddenly through a gap in the hills they are looking down, across precipitous miles, at the Lake of Galilee where it forms a blue floor at the bottom of the plain. And this time she says, "Ha-yam [the sea]; say 'Yam,' Jesus." Or she takes him with her in the cool of the evening when she carries a jug to draw water at the spring outside the town. There is only one spring at Nazareth, and it is still called the Fountain of the Virgin, after her. And this time she says, "Ha-'en [the spring]; say ''En,' Jesus." So the mind-pictures of the Incarnate were formed; and when he preached, years later, about a city set on a hill, or fishermen casting their nets into the sea, or a spring of water welling up to eternal life, he was utilizing the wisdom he had learned from that wise playmate of his, long ago.

When our thoughts go back to our Blessed Lady in the stable at Bethlehem, we picture her as protecting us; that is quite right. When they go back to our Blessed Lady standing by the Cross on Calvary, we picture her as pitying us; that is quite right too. But sometimes, let us think of our Blessed Lady by the well at Nazareth, as playing with us. I dare say you are wondering why, all through this sermon, I have been mixing up two ideas which are very different in your mind, the idea of acquiring wisdom, which to you means class, and the idea of playing, which to you means break. I don't know, are they really so very different? I expect you know what is the derivation of the word "school"? It comes from a Greek word which means "waste of time." After all, work and play, play and work, are all part of the same thing; they are all part of growing up, of turning into the kind of people we are going to be. And either of them is incomplete if you are left entirely to yourself. You don't get much out of being left alone with a book, if there is no one about to tell you which parts of the book matter, and explain the difficulties to you. You don't get much fun out of playing if you are left hour after hour to yourself; you can't enjoy enjoyment properly unless there is somebody to share it with. So my best wish for you is that our Blessed Lady, the reflection and the counterpart of that Divine Wisdom which played over the earth when God made it, should be your companion. We imitate the activities of Almighty God by making mountains, but we make them out of molehills. We mope and get depressed when things don't go according to schedule; as if anything in this world ever did go according to schedule, or was meant to, for long. We need, so often, the tender mockery of her smile, the reassuring pressure of her hand.

CHAPTER 4

The Boast of an Apostle

You find it easy to be patient with the vanity of others, you who are so full of good sense. Why, you let other people tyrannize over you, prey upon you, take advantage of you, vaunt their power over you, browbeat you! I say this without taking credit to myself, I say it as if we had had no power to play such a part; yet in fact—here my vanity speaks—I can claim all that others claim. Are they Hebrews? So am I. Are they Israelites? So am I. Are they descended from Abraham? So am I. Are they Christ's servants? These are wild words; I am something more. I have toiled harder, spent longer days in prison, been beaten so cruelly, so often looked death in the face. Five times the Jews scourged me, and spared me but one lash in the forty; three times I was beaten with rods, once I was stoned; I have been shipwrecked three times, I have spent a night and a day as a castaway at sea. What journeys I have undertaken, in danger from rivers, in danger from robbers, in danger from my own people, in danger from the Gentiles; danger in cities, danger in the wilderness, danger in the sea, danger among false brethren! I have met with toil and weariness, so often been sleepless, hungry and thirsty; so often denied myself food, gone cold and naked. And all this, over and above something else which I do not count; I mean the burden I carry every day, my anxious care for all the

RONALD KNOX

churches; does anyone feel a scruple? I share it; is anyone's conscience hurt? I am ablaze with indignation. If I must needs boast, I will boast of the things which humiliate me; the God who is Father of our Lord Jesus Christ, blessed be his name for ever, knows that I am telling the truth. When I was at Damascus, the agent of King Aretas was keeping guard over the city of the Damascenes, intent on seizing me, and to escape from his hands I had to be let down through a window along the wall, in a hamper.

If we are to boast (although boasting is out of place), I will go on to the visions and revelations the Lord has granted me. There is a man I know who was carried out of himself in Christ, fourteen years since; was his spirit in his body? I cannot tell. Was it apart from his body? I cannot tell; God knows. This man, at least, was carried up into the third heaven. I can only tell you that this man, with his spirit in his body, or with his spirit apart from his body, God knows which, not I, was carried up into Paradise, and heard mysteries which man is not allowed to utter. That is the man about whom I will boast; I will not boast about myself, except to tell you of my humiliations. It would not be vanity, if I had a mind to boast about such a man as that; I should only be telling the truth. But I will spare you the telling of it; I have no mind that anybody should think of me except as he sees me, as he hears me talking to him. And indeed, for fear that these surpassing revelations should make me proud, I was given a sting to distress my outward nature, an angel of Satan sent to rebuff me. Three times it made me entreat the Lord to rid me of it; but he told me, My grace is enough for thee; my strength finds its full scope in thy weakness. More than ever, then, I delight to boast of the weaknesses that humiliate me, so that the strength of Christ may enshrine itself in me. (2 COR. 11:19–33, 12:1–9)

The Gospel in Slow Motion

THIS PASSAGE COMES FROM ST. PAUL'S SECOND LETTER TO the Corinthians; and they had written back to him in between his first and second to them. (That would do for point one, wouldn't it, "Always answer your letters.") But whereas it's fairly easy to see, from St. Paul's first letter to them, what their first letter to him was about, St. Paul's second letter to them is, I think, one of the obscurest documents in the world, and heaven only knows what their second letter to him can have been about. They were angry with him for not having come to pay them a visit when he had told them that he meant to. And so they wrote and criticized his conduct; or perhaps they simply wrote and repeated other people's criticisms of his conduct. But, you know, repeating other people's criticisms is often almost as bad as making criticisms of one's own. There isn't always a great deal of difference between saying "Your ears are too large," and saying "Do you know, Selina's been going about saying your ears are too large; isn't it beastly of her?" The fact is, I'm afraid, that the Church at Corinth was very much split up into factions; and the chief thing they quarrelled about was whether St. Paul was the last word in apostles or not. Some said he was; others said no, other missionaries were much more imposing; look at Apollos, now! [Apollos was a missionary who had come along to Corinth after St. Paul founded the Church there, and had somehow made himself a party in it.] "Paul is always writing you long letters, which you find very impressive, but when you actually see him you find he's a rather insignificant little man, not nearly such a good preacher as Apollos..." and so on.

And so on and so on. It isn't at all clear what they had been saying about St. Paul; but in this letter he is evidently out to correct their impressions. He does it in a very vague, allusive way, for ten chapters or so, and then, in this present passage, he really lets them have it. He says he is not going to boast, but really of course he has to. There are certain occasions when you can't say what you want to say without boasting rather; like Bishop Ullathorne, when somebody asked him what was the best book on humility and he said, "Best book on 'umility? I wrote it myself." St. Paul couldn't meet all these criticisms which were directed entirely at himself, without talking about himself and pointing out that he was rather a fine chap. He hated doing that, because he wasn't only a very good Christian, he was also a tremendous gentleman, St. Paul, and he felt it was bad form to boast of what he'd done. So he keeps on, in the first place, apologizing for boasting, and, in the second place, trying to talk not so much about the things he's done as the things he's had to put up with. "You say I'm not much of an apostle?" (that's his line), "Well, if I'm not, why does Providence always give me such a raw deal? Do you think I lead my present kind of life for fun?"

He doesn't start off by saying, "You suffer fools gladly, seeing that you yourselves are wise, for you suffer if a man bring you into bondage, if a man devour you, if a man take from you" and all the rest of it, as the old translation has it; what would be the sense of writing down all that nonsense? No, he starts off, "If so many others boast of their natural advantages, I must be allowed to boast too. [Here our passage begins.] You find it easy to be patient with the vanity of others, you who are so full of good sense! [That is sarcastic.] Why, you let other people tyrannize over you, prey upon you, take advantage of you, vaunt their power over you, browbeat you!" I think it's clear that among the other nasty things which had

The Gospel in Slow Motion

been said about St. Paul by his enemies they had said he was always talking about himself, always trying to give a good account of himself. So he starts off, you see, "Boast, do I? Well, what about these other people? Look at them throwing their weight about! Look at the way they try to run the show at Corinth—won't let you call your souls your own!" What he's thinking of mostly, I fancy, is that other missionaries lived at the expense of the faithful, as they had a perfect right to do, but perhaps some of them lived a little too well at the expense of the faithful. St. Paul always made a point of carrying on his trade—he was a tentmaker, as you know—so that there shouldn't have to be any second collection for the holy man's breakfast. "I say this without taking credit to myself," he adds, "as though we had no power to play such a part; yet in fact—here my vanity speaks—I can claim all that others claim." When he says, "I speak as a fool," that's what it means; he means "this is a bit of vanity on my part." And so he goes on to give his credentials; to show that he is really an apostle just as much as the other people, more than the other people.

Why he lays stress on being a Jew, I don't know; perhaps because Apollos was a Jew (so the Acts tells us) who was learned in the scriptures; perhaps people had been saying, "It takes a Jew, a man like Apollos, to comment on scripture properly." Nor do I know why he says, "Are they Christ's servants?" I think it was probably a title which these rival teachers used—"So-and-so, the deacon of Christ." Anyhow, he's not going to let them get away with it; "these are wild words, I am something more." And he breaks out into that long catalogue of discomforts and persecutions; if this isn't being an apostle, what is? The imprisonments, the beatings, the stonings, the shipwrecks, the constant travelling, with its various dangers. It was very tiring being an apostle—more tiring than pulling potatoes; it made you very hungry—more hungry than waiting for your turn in refectory; it made you very cold—colder than practising in the recreation room. The first and most obvious way of testing whether a man is really an apostle of Christ (he implies) is to find out just how much discomfort he's prepared to put up with in order to claim the title.

Then he switches off on to a quite different point, at the tail of the list. "And all this, over and above something else which I do not count; I mean the burden I carry every day, my anxious care for all the churches." The second test of whether a man is really a good apostle is how much he worries; how much the misbehaviour of Christians, at Corinth for example, gives him sleepless nights. "And," says St. Paul, "*I* mind about these things terribly.... Does anyone feel a scruple? I share it. Is anyone's conscience hurt? I am ablaze with indignation." He's desperately anxious not to boast, you see; he won't say, "I have a burning zeal for the honour of God which can't bear any scandal in the Church. He represents himself rather as a sort of fussy old gentleman who must always be writing to the *Times* when things happen that he doesn't approve of. "So humiliating for me," he says, "isn't it, that I should mind so terribly about these things?"

"Yes," he goes on, "if I must needs boast, I will boast of the things which humiliate me." And then he goes on to tell them the story about his stay in Damascus, just after he became a Christian, and how the place got too hot to hold him. "The agent of King Aretas was keeping guard over the city of the Damascenes, intent to seize

The Gospel in Slow Motion

me." You'll find they get that wrong in all the books. They call this gentleman "the governor of the city under King Aretas"; he wasn't anything of the sort; Damascus didn't belong to King Aretas then. No, he was a kind of consul that looked after the interests of a hairy old sheik out in the desert; I imagine him sitting in his office in his shirt-sleeves with a gang of "boys," kind of gunmen, who were ready to bump off anybody he didn't like. And the Jews gave him a tip of sorts, and he undertook that when St. Paul next went out of the city gates there would be somebody waiting for him with a piece of lead piping tied up in a stocking, and that would be the last that would be heard of St. Paul. However, the secret got out, and the disciples put St. Paul in a large basket and let him down over the wall. Why does he tell us that story just here? I think, because it humiliates him; he didn't cut a very heroic figure, twisting round and round on a rope, disguised as old clothes. "I didn't half look a fool," he says; "but do you know, I am rather proud of looking that kind of fool."

By now, he's more or less come to the conclusion that you can't avoid boasting when you're writing a letter like this to people like this. Evidently one of the nasty things they had been saying about St. Paul was that he didn't have ecstasies. That may sound rather a mild form of criticism. But I think at Corinth, just then, they had all rather lost their heads over what were known in the early Church as "spiritual gifts"; we shall be talking more about them next Sunday. And I think you can imagine some acid old lady in Christian Corinth saying, "My dear, he may be all you say, but I can't feel that he's a very *spiritual* man." There may be more to it than that. I was telling you just now that the main reason why certain people at Corinth were angry with St. Paul was because he had cried off paying them a visit, after announcing his intention of doing so. They seem to have thought this showed a kind of flightiness about St. Paul—he was the kind of person who said Yes one day and No the next. And you'll find in the Acts that when he proposed to make this visit it is described in an odd way: "Paul put it in the Spirit to go through Macedonia and Achaea." It's a strange phrase, but it possibly means that he got a sort of divine inspiration that it would be a good thing to do. Well, if he first wrote and said, "The Holy Spirit has told me that I must come and visit you," and then later he wrote and said, "I'm sorry I shan't be visiting you after all, because I've got too much work to do here, at Ephesus," the Corinthians would think he was playing fast and loose with the divine guidance. "Not a very spiritual man, my dear."

For whatever reason, he decided he'd got to show them he *was* a spiritual man; and so he gives them that odd, breathless account of his great ecstasy: "There is a man I know who was carried out of himself in Christ fourteen years since; was his spirit in his body? I cannot tell. Was it apart from his body? I cannot tell; God knows. This man, at least, was carried up into the third heaven. I can only tell you that this man, with his spirit in his body or with his spirit apart from his body, God knows which, not I, was carried up into Paradise, and heard mysteries which man is not allowed to utter." You see how shy he is about the whole thing; he won't be questioned about what state he was in or what it was he heard; he only knows, in a quite matter-of-fact way, that he was taken up to Paradise. And although it was obviously himself, he talks about it all as if it was somebody else; like a very shy young flying officer telling the story of some feat of his and putting it all down to "a chap I know."

The Gospel in Slow Motion

Then, rather confusingly, he says, "That is the person I'm going to boast about; I'm not going to boast about myself." At first sight, that sounds a bit thin. It sounds rather like what Cicero, in one of his works on rhetoric, calls *praetermissio*. The art of *praetermissio* is to bring in a lot of facts by explaining that you are not going to bring them in. "I shall not say a word about your having cheated at cards; I shall not shock the ears of this audience by describing the way in which you rifled your mother's tomb; wild horses wouldn't drag out of me any allusion to the fact that you were sacked by three successive employers for stealing the petty cash"—that is *praetermissio*. Is St. Paul using the same dodge here? No; when he says he is going to boast about a man being carried up into Paradise, but is not going to boast about himself, what he means is that he doesn't particularly regard it as a feather in his cap having been taken up to Paradise. It might have been anybody else, not he. He merely registers the fact as a fact; he is not going to boast about it, because he had done nothing to deserve it.

And indeed, for fear he *should* be inclined to boast about it, God sent him a mortification of some kind which he calls a stake, or pointed pole, in connection with his flesh. What that was, nobody knows. The modern pious books mostly tell you it was a temptation. The modern Protestant scholars tell you it was an illness; malaria perhaps, or epilepsy. The early Fathers of the Church thought, and I think, that it means persecution; persecution at the hands of the Jews, his fellow-countrymen, whom he describes here, as in a passage of his letter to the Romans, as his "flesh," his own flesh and blood. Wherever he started a really successful mission, the Jews followed him up and tried to spoil the effect of it, because they hated him so. Whatever the true explanation is, the point of the story is that he asked to have this mortification taken away from him, and God refused. Paul's weakness must be made perfect through God's strength; he must learn not to depend on himself, for all his heroic labours, for all the spiritual privileges he enjoyed. And that will do as a moral to end up with. No work you ever do for God will be worth boasting about. No state of prayer you ever reach will be a reason for patting yourself on the back, or turning up your nose at other people. Your work will have real value, your prayer will be really useful, to yourself and to others, in so far as you learn to leave everything to God and let his Spirit work in you, his strength make itself perfect in your weakness.

CHAPTER 5

How to Assert Ourselves

Live in harmony of mind, falling in with the opinions of common folk, instead of following conceited thoughts; never give yourselves airs of wisdom.

Do not repay injury with injury; study your behaviour in the world's sight as well as in God's. Keep peace with all men, where it is possible, for your part. Do not avenge yourselves, beloved; allow retribution to run its course; so we read in scripture, Vengeance is for me, I will repay, says the Lord. Rather, feed thy enemy if he is hungry, give him drink if he is thirsty; by doing this, thou wilt heap coals of fire upon his head. Do not be disarmed by malice; disarm malice with kindness. (ROM. 12:16–21)

I THINK YOU CAN TELL FROM ALL HIS WRITINGS THAT ST. Paul was a very sensitive man, and felt injuries very deeply. Not so much injuries which affected himself; at least, I expect he did feel these, too, deeply; but he realized that he mustn't mind—if people defied his authority, or spoke contemptuously about him, who was he that he should be offended by it? *He* wasn't important; *his* dignity didn't matter. No, but when people tried to undermine all the work he had been doing by telling his converts at Corinth, or in Galatia, "Paul has got the gospel all wrong, it isn't a bit like that really"—then, to the end of his life, St. Paul did flare up; he couldn't help it. He was a man full of zeal for the truth as he saw it; he couldn't sit down quietly and shrug his shoulders over it when people attacked the principles that were dear to him. And that helps us to understand why St. Paul, before his conversion, was such a bitter persecutor of the Christian Church. The very quality that made him afterwards such a splendid champion of the faith, made him a cruel enemy of the faith until he learned to believe in it himself. And, as a young man—when we are young, our impatient zeal often takes ugly forms—he wasn't content to *feel* angry with the Christians; he went for them. He made his way into house after house, carrying men and women off, and committing them to prison. These people were insulting God and his law and his temple, and Paul wasn't going to sit down under it.

He only learned later on, only learned when he was a Christian, the lesson which you get in today's epistle, "Vengeance is for me, I will repay, says the Lord." It comes in the Old Testament, but the Jews never took much notice of it, and Christians haven't always taken as much notice of it as they ought to have. I always liked a story which I think I either read in one of Maurice Baring's books, or heard from Maurice Baring himself, about an obscure Russian village before the great Revolution in Russia, when they all went atheist. There were a good many atheists already going about in Russia, and one of these came to a remote village somewhere and made a speech on the village green. "Now," he said, "I am going to curse God. And if there is a God, obviously he will kill me for being

The Gospel in Slow Motion

so impious." And then he cursed God, and nothing happened, and he said to the villagers, "There, you see, he didn't kill me." And the villagers said, "No, but we will," and they did. We are always so anxious, aren't we, to get quick results? And God takes his time, and we get impatient, and take the business out of his hands—his own business of judging men and punishing them for the offences which they commit against him; or against ourselves. We are not too keen on people committing offences against ourselves.

When I say that, I don't mean that law-courts are all wrong, and the sentences inflicted by judges on burglars and people who drive on the right-hand side of the road are all wrong. There has to be human justice. But human justice should never be merely vindictive; we punish our fellow-human beings not merely to annoy them, but either because we hope it will do them good, or because it is not safe to leave them at large, or, anyhow, so as to make other people see that it doesn't pay, doing that kind of thing. Only God can *avenge* wrong-doing: I mean, only God has a *right* to avenge wrong-doing. We can see that when we meet a vindictive person; it makes you feel sick to hear somebody else say, "I'm going to pay her out one of these days." But when the grievance is your own, it's not so easy to realize that vindictiveness is wrong.

Well then, you say, what ought I to do when somebody does me a bad turn? Just take no notice, and pretend it hasn't happened? No, that's not the idea. St. Paul goes on to explain about that. "If thy enemy be hungry, give him food, if he be thirsty, give him drink; by doing so thou wilt heap coals of fire on his head." Notice that St. Paul is still quoting from the Old Testament. There's nothing particularly Christian about the sentiment; it comes from the book of Proverbs. It isn't quite clear how the coals of fire come in. Some think King Solomon meant, "Treat your enemies with all possible kindness, and then God will be so pleased with *you* that he will arrange for quite appalling calamities to happen to your enemies, so that you will score in the long run." That, as you will see, is not a very Christian point of view. I doubt if it was what King Solomon meant, and I am quite certain it is not what St. Paul meant. There's another explanation suggested by St. Augustine; he thinks that if you do good to your enemies they will be so ashamed of themselves they will feel hot all over; the coals of fire are merely an expression for that sense of wanting to sink into the earth which I hope we've all felt before now when we realized that we'd behaved really badly. That may be so, but I confess it sounds to me a rather priggish motive for wanting to be kind to our enemies. I mean, it's rather a priggish attitude to go to bed saying to yourself, "Gosh, how mean that girl will feel when she finds I've mended her stockings for her!" No, I think it is just a piece of paradox. Your instinct is to feel that you will have asserted yourself properly if you smash the person who has annoyed you. Whereas really you only assert yourself properly when you forgive the person who annoys you. To forgive is one of the highest privileges man can attain. But you can't forgive until somebody has offended you. Somebody *has* offended you? What fun—now's your chance to do some forgiving. The Christian's form of revenge is to return good for evil.

Why was St. Paul specially anxious to rub that in, when he was writing to the Romans? Why did he say, just before, "Keep peace with all men, where it is possible, for your part"? Were the Christians at Rome a particularly quarrelsome set of people? No, I think his point is rather different. We know that, a year or two before, the Jews had been expelled from Rome by an edict of the Emperor Claudius; St. Paul met two of these refugees, called Aquila and Priscilla, at Corinth. But in this epistle to the Romans he sends his greetings to Aquila and Priscilla, so it is clear that they had just got back. Well, Jews aren't always very popular, you know, among working people. And when any Government takes action against the Jews, it isn't long before the neighbours start breaking their windows. So I imagine that when people like Aquila and Priscilla got back to Rome, they would find the Gentiles who lived near them hadn't been idle. The door-scraper would be gone, and the neighbours' hens would be all over the back garden, and the neighbours would have thrown all their pots and pans there and turned it into an ash-pit. So you can imagine Priscilla saying to Aquila, "I hear it was that nasty little bandy-legged boy of Phormio's that scrawled up those rude remarks on the back door while we were away; I wonder what'll be the best way of getting even with him?" And then they go to church, and they are delighted to hear that a letter is going to be read out from St. Paul at Corinth: "Dear Paul, how delightful to get news of him! And how splendid to hear about all the people at Corinth." And then the letter is read out, and it says, "If it be possible, as much as lies in you, be at peace with all men. Don't repay evil for evil. Vengeance belongs to God. If you really want to score off your enemy, feed him when he's hungry, give him drink when he's thirsty." So Aquila and Priscilla go home, and have to give the bandy-legged Phormio boy a new top; it is the Christian's revenge.

How does all this apply to ourselves? There are three separate hints St. Paul gives us about our behaviour, in the course of this very short epistle; and they are all worth considering. One is when he says, "Study your behaviour in the world's sight as well as in God's." The old translation has "providing good things," which is a bad translation; it sounds as if it meant sending for buns from the confectioner's. No, "Study your behaviour, in the world's sight as well as in God's." We Christian people have got to set an example to our neighbours; we are servants of the patient Christ, and of his gentle Mother, and if we don't show patience and gentleness, the world will think there is very little good in being a Christian. And then, "Keep peace with all men, where it is possible, for your part." You can't prevent other people being odious to you, but it takes two to make a quarrel—don't let the odiousness be on your side, don't give the other party an excuse for being odious, even by tiresome, annoying little ways. Have peace with all men—how difficult! And perhaps having peace with all women is, shall we say, equally difficult. If it be possible—it isn't always possible; we had to fight Hitler, when goodness knows we didn't want to. And you won't always be able to live at peace; circumstances will crop up in which you will have to get across other people, in standing up for religion or for common decency; but *where* it's possible, have peace. And especially when you are all living herded together like this, and the snow and the slush doesn't make it easy for you to avoid one another's society, have peace; don't start trouble. And then, the third point, if trouble does start, don't revenge yourself. The Latin, you know, is even stronger than that; it makes out the meaning to be, "Don't stand up in your own defence," don't try to justify yourself, even. Anyhow, the point is the same; we've got to fight down, whenever it bobs up, that spirit of self-assertion, of taking our own dignity seriously, which there is in all of us. The *Imitation of Christ*, which knows a lot about human nature, says that when we have a grievance we generally pretend to ourselves that we wouldn't mind if it wasn't that particular person—a ghastly little beast like that! Which shows, you see, that it's just our self-conceit that has been wounded; we want to assert ourselves somehow. Assert yourself? Assert yourself by all means, says St. Paul; why not heap coals of fire on the other person's head by being specially nice to them? That will assert your *true* self; the self that is to be Christ.

CHAPTER 6

A Saint of Last Century

I will make of thee a great nation. (GEN. 12:2)

THIS AFTERNOON LET'S TALK ABOUT A GREAT CATHOLIC educator, St. John Bosco, who founded the Salesian order. I thought you would like to be told about him, partly because, as saints go, he is a modern one; if he had been born two months earlier, he would have been alive when the battle of Waterloo was fought, and if he had lived a month longer, he would have been alive when I was born. Partly because he is one of those nice human saints who aren't all ecstasies and hairshirt; he did rather eccentric things and had rather odd experiences, such as you don't get in most lives of most saints, though perhaps that was partly because most lives of most saints are rather stupidly written. Anyhow, whoever wrote his life I think Don Bosco—that was the name he was always known by before he was canonized—would seem an unusual figure.

He was born of peasant parents in a small village in Lombardy; it looked as if he was going to spend all his life minding the cattle, and his eldest brother, who was only a half-brother, was determined that he should. But from the first he wanted to be a priest, and, like several other saints, he rather played at being a priest when he was quite small. St. John Vianney, the other great priest-saint of the nineteenth century, used to collect his small friends and get them to say the rosary with him at improvised altars out in the country, while they were looking after sheep. St. John Bosco, who was like St. John Vianney in many ways—he too is a saint of the confessional, he too could read men's hearts, he too was kept awake night after night by the devil—St. John Bosco was more of a publicist than St. John Vianney. He used to collect a crowd in the village, not only of children but of grown-ups, every Sunday, and treat them to a performance which began with the rosary and ended with a shortened edition, which he himself supplied from memory, of the curé's sermon that morning. Which is the first point at which St. John Bosco is a good example to us. Point one: always listen to sermons.

How did he manage that? I mean, when you've got a hard Sunday behind you, the rosary isn't everybody's money, and lots of people are content to have heard the sermon only once. No, it was the middle part of the performance which was the jam in the middle of the sandwich; this small boy had a tightrope stretched between two trees in the family orchard, and he had taught himself to walk on it. He had also taught himself conjuring, and used to keep the villagers gaping by producing rabbits out of hats and all the rest of it. You see what a very nineteenth-century saint he was. St. Joseph of Cupertino would have found it very easy to walk on a tightrope, because he was always being levitated; indeed, you may almost say his difficulty was to keep on the ground. And that would have made it easy to walk on a tightrope, but it wouldn't have been quite fair, would it? St. John Bosco played the game, there was nothing supernatural about his tightrope; indeed, from one end of his life to the other he never had, so far as is known, any ecstasies or any levitations. He did do miracles later on, lots and lots of them; but as a small boy he was content to do sham miracles, by fetching rabbits out of top-hats. And the lesson of that is, I think, that we should all do our best to cultivate the special gifts God has given us. Because you can't be a tightrope walker or a conjurer unless you've got a sort of natural gift for it; and it's not a gift which seems at first sight to have much to do with being a priest. But St. John Bosco's job, all his life, was to win the confidence of ragged boys and make them attached to him, and juggling and things like that are very useful if you want to establish contact with the young, when they are rather shy of you. So that's the second point: don't neglect the special gift God has given you, even if it's only playing the piano; you never know when it may come in useful.

Well, it would take too long to tell you about all the difficulties he had in becoming a priest. But there's one thing I must tell you about his boyhood before we get on to the main activities of his life; when he was nine years old he dreamt one night that he was in the middle of a crowd of children who, I am sorry to say, were all shouting and yelling. It's the kind of dream that ordinarily comes not to small boys or small girls, but to elderly schoolmasters or schoolmistresses who have eaten something that disagreed with them before they went to bed. But St. John Bosco, all through his life, had dreams which were useful to him; he was such a busy man that he couldn't afford to be idle even in his sleep. On this occasion, in his dream, he tried to stop the other children making a noise by beating them. But a complete stranger came up to him, in his dream, and said, "Don't do that; be gentle with them, if you want to win their friendship." So St. John took that to heart, and later on, when he had quantities of small boys to look after, he always followed that rule. I'm not going to draw any moral from that, or you would start bringing it up the next time you have a row with your form mistress; so we'll go on to when St. John Bosco became a priest.

He started as a priest in Turin; which was, and I fancy still is, a pretty beastly sort of manufacturing town. They were the sort of people who worked in factories and got bad wages, and were mostly rather revolutionary and anticlerical. Also, in those days there was an obscure Protestant sect, the Waldensian sect, which used to try and turn people into Protestants by giving them plenty of soup and so on, largely I'm afraid with money supplied to them from England; and they were rather strong in Turin. But what worried St. John most was the condition of the young men and boys there; young men who had come in from the country to work in factories, and had no decent places to live in; boys who were orphans or neglected by their parents, who wandered about the town playing pitch-and-toss and learning to beg. The climax came in an odd way: St. John went into a church to say Mass when he wasn't expected, and the sacristan got hold of a small boy who was fooling about the church and said, "You can serve the father's Mass." To which the boy replied, "No, I can't, because I don't know how." And the sacristan, who I suppose hadn't had any memorable dreams at the age of nine, got hold of a broomstick and started chivying the boy out of the church. St. John interfered, and that was how he came to hear the story; so he got the boy to wait till after Mass, and then,

The Gospel in Slow Motion

after kneeling down and saying a Hail Mary with him, he started giving him an instruction, and teaching him how to say his prayers, which he'd also forgotten how to do. That will do for point three: get Mother Clare to teach you how to answer Mass.

That was on the feast of the Immaculate Conception 1841; and this boy brought half a dozen of his friends to see Don Bosco, and then *they* brought *their* friends, and the whole thing went on like a snowball, till the Saint was followed everywhere by a crowd of ragamuffins whom he tried to attach to himself, giving them buns at intervals and teaching them their catechism. And after a bit it looked as if he would have to establish some kind of headquarters for this strange apostolate. It was just a hundred years ago that St. John was appointed chaplain to an orphanage, and there was a derelict passage there in which the boys were allowed to play, and two rooms were knocked into one another to make a chapel for them—by now they numbered a hundred and fifty. It all looked all right, and you'd hardly believe what happened—the neighbours began to complain of the noise. It's an extraordinary thing about elderly people, that the sound of a large number of childish voices all shouting "*Last bell!*" at the same moment puts them in a bad humour. So St. John had to leave; and the same happened at the next place they tried, and the next—St. John had no money at all, so he could only get these stray shelters out of charity; and at one time they were reduced to having an open-air picnic in the country every Sunday, and St. John used to hear their confessions sitting on a hummock in the middle of a field. But when winter came this wouldn't work, so St. John had somehow to raise the sum of twelve pounds, for which he managed to rent a disused hayloft, which thus became the first real home of St. John Bosco and the Salesian order in general. By now, I should mention, the number of boys had risen to four hundred.

The curious thing about St. John was that he never worried about these momentary setbacks, because he always had clearly mapped out in his mind a picture of what his future premises were going to be like. "Soon," he used to say, "we shall have churches, playgrounds, and houses, priests, clerics and laymen to help us bring up the boys, and we shall have thousands of boys." He would point up in the air with his stick to the exact place where, later on, the statue of our Lady was going to stand at the top of the main tower. The fact that he had no money at all didn't make any difference, because all his life he trusted absolutely in Providence. Later on, he was to revive the miracle of the five thousand, just as St. John Vianney did; by actual count, he fed three hundred boys on fifteen rolls, which were all still left there at the end. And that will do for point four, which is the moral of all the saints' biographies: trust madly in Providence as long as you feel sure you are doing the right thing with your life.

It didn't impress everybody like that; St. John's clerical colleagues got worried about the way he was spending himself on daydreams, and at last came to the conclusion that he was mad. Two canons of the diocese called on him officially one day, with a cab outside to take him to the asylum, which was fortunately quite close. And they got him talking, and egged him on to tell them about the gorgeous buildings he was going to put up and the great order he was going to found, and then they asked him to come out for a drive. St. John spotted exactly what was up, so when they got

The Gospel in Slow Motion

outside the front door he made them get into the carriage first; oh, he couldn't possibly go in front of a canon; and when they were inside he slammed the door and told the cabman to take them off to the asylum; there wasn't a moment to be lost. So by the time they reached the asylum they were hanging out of the windows, purple in the face, trying to get the cabman to go back; and of course they were immediately locked up, and it took some time before the chaplain came along and recognized them and they were let out. Chesterton has a story very much like that somewhere, I think in a book called *The Return of Don Quixote*; but it really happened to St. John Bosco. And that will do for point five: always let other people go through the door first.

Well, of course it all went all right; by begging money and by running lotteries and by every means he could think of short of forgery and stealing, St. John got his money, and built the enormous establishment which I'm afraid you won't see if you go to Turin now, because I rather think we have bombed it all down. He had plenty of adventures; because the anti-clericals didn't like him and the Waldenses didn't like him, and several times they tried to bump him off. It really wasn't safe for him to go to a sick call, because it generally turned out to be an ambush of his enemies. There was one rather lonely walk he had to take fairly often at night, the sort of place where undesirable people hung about. One autumn evening, just as he got there, an enormous mastiff came sidling up to him; and St. John, who liked animals, tickled it under the throat and all that, and it followed him all the way home, and the same thing happened every time he took that walk, till one night when two thugs, put up to it I'm afraid by the Waldensians, suddenly threw a sack over his head in the darkness. And it looked as if it was all up with Don Bosco, when suddenly there was a hideous growl in the background, and there was one of the thugs running for his life, while the other was pinned to the ground with the mastiff at his throat. That will do for point six: always make friends with dogs.

Well, I've hardly started telling you anything about St. John; how he used to remind people in the confessional of the sins they had left out; how he sometimes had a dream at night which told him the exact state of conscience of every boy in the building; how for two years the devil kept worrying him by making noises and throwing things about in his bedroom, making noises so horrible that people listening at the door ran away in terror. I haven't told you of the printing-press he ran, and the enormous amount of cheap pious books and parish magazines he turned out; all rather bad stuff, I imagine, but useful, and St. John didn't mind as long as he was being useful. How he was the close friend of two Popes, and yet all the time he managed to keep on good terms, personally, with anti-clerical leaders like Cavour; how he went to Paris and took Paris by storm, and very nearly succeeded in converting Victor Hugo. By the time he died, at the age of seventy-three, there were a hundred thousand people at his funeral, and there were already two hundred and fifty Salesian houses scattered about the world, looking after a hundred and thirty thousand children and turning out eighteen thousand skilled mechanics of various kinds every year. And what he said about it himself was this: "If our Lord could have found a more wretched instrument than me to carry out his work, he would have chosen that instrument rather than me, and

The Gospel in Slow Motion

he would have been better served." There is point seven, an obvious one: ask God for the grace of humility.

There are seven points from St. John's life for you; you can try to repeat them in the dormitory if you like, but don't start walking the tightrope.

CHAPTER 7

The Weed Killer

And he put before them another parable; Here is an image, he said, of the kingdom of heaven. There was a man who sowed his field with clean seed; but while all the world was asleep, an enemy of his came and scattered tares among the wheat, and was gone. So, when the blade had sprung up and come into ear, the tares, too, came to light; and the farmer's men went to him and said, Sir, was it not clean seed thou didst sow in thy field? How comes it, then, that there are tares in it? He said, An enemy has done it. And his men asked him, Wouldst thou then have us go and gather them up? But he said, No; or perhaps while you are gathering the tares you will root up the wheat with them. Leave them to grow side by side till harvest, and when harvest-time comes I will give the word to the reapers, Gather up the tares first, and tie them in bundles to be burned, and store the wheat in my barn. (MATT. 13:24–30)

THIS STORY, LIKE MOST OF THE STORIES OUR LORD TOLD, doesn't need much altering to make it a thing of here and now. You can even imagine it happening to yourself. Suppose, for example, that you were a German spy; and a message came to you from

RONALD KNOX

Germany in secret cipher, "Sabotage farm at Aldenham stop most important stop especially wheat in park stop." That's the way official people send telegrams to one another. Well, there are all sorts of sabotage that you might go in for: leaving the gates open so that the cattle get loose and eat the yew-berries, which are very bad for them; or climbing through fences so that the sheep can get out; or setting Mr. S.'s alarm-clock wrong so that he doesn't get up at the right time; all sorts of ways. And there are all sorts of ways in which you might sabotage the wheat in the park; but one way would be the way it was done in our Lord's parable. Don't start this term; the thing's got to be done at night, and the nights are very cold just now. Wait till next term, and then choose a fine night and climb out of your dormitory by the magnolia tree, if it hasn't come off altogether by then, and take with you the seed of some plant that isn't wheat, but grows faster than wheat. It says cockle in our Bible, but it isn't really certain what stuff it was the man used; cockle is rather a jolly blue flower. I'll tell you what you might do: get hold of some seed of those lupins that grow just outside the chapel door; they grow very fast, and they are a kind of crop really. You'd want a good deal; and you'd have to take it down with you night after night in a bag, and sow it all over where the wheat is sown. And then you would slink back and snuggle up in bed, and nobody would be any the wiser. Unless you caught a cold; of course that would be awful, and probably give the whole show away.

Well, before long those lupins would begin to come up, and cause a good deal of surprise. Mr. S. would go to Mr. V., just like the men in the parable, and say, "Looks to me like we didn't sow clean seed in the park." And Mr. V. would take off his hat and scratch

The Gospel in Slow Motion

his head just like the man in the parable, and say, "Tell you what it is—an enemy has done this, see?" And then what would happen? Well, I suppose the Ministry of Agriculture would have to give leave for the wheat to be cut early, as they did when the vetch came up among the wheat out in the top field two years ago. Otherwise, it might be arranged that everybody should set to work grubbing up the lupin at once. But that would take a lot of time, and if you had been clever the roots of the lupin might be all mixed up with the wheat, so that you couldn't pull up one without pulling up the other. And yet if the lupins were left to grow mixed up with the wheat, the combine might thrash them all together, and our bread would have a very funny taste. When my sisters were at school, one of them wrote home and referred to "the stuff they call bread." I'm sure you wouldn't do that, because you're much better behaved than my sisters were; but you'd feel tempted to, if the bread was all full of lupins.

What did the farmer do in the story? Well, of course, he didn't use a combine; all the reaping was done by hand, and so he arranged that the wheat and the cockle should be collected separately; the wheat would be put away in the Dutch barn, and the cockle would be burnt where it lay, making a lovely smoke and smell. And that, our Lord says, is like the kingdom of heaven. Mankind, in this world, is a very mixed crop; there are a great many weeds about, and so much mixed up with the true grain that it's almost impossible now for us to tell them apart. But wait till the day of judgement. Then the just (please God, that means you and me) will shine forth in the kingdom of their father, and the other people will get what they deserve. God will be able to decide, easily enough, which were the people who pulled long faces and looked good and were really hypocrites all the time—he won't get them mixed up with the wheat. And he will be able to decide which were the people who really did their best, although temptation was always getting the better of them and pulling them down, fought a losing battle all their lives and went to prison and were generally thought, here on earth, to have made a mess of their lives, but they did their best, all the time, and he will know that they were true grain.

That's a parable which you can apply in more ways than one. It is a comforting parable, when you are feeling rather depressed about the condition of the world at large. Couldn't God interfere somehow? Couldn't he send us a convenient epidemic, typhoid or something of that kind, which would neatly kill off all the people who seem to us to be doing so much harm in the world, and leave all the nice people immune? The answer to that is that in the long run it doesn't frightfully matter who wins and who loses in these earthly debates which we consider so important. What matters is not whether So-and-so gets away with it now, but whether he is going to get away with it at the last judgement, with all eternity in front of him. Go out into the park next summer, when the wheat has grown, and lie down on your stomach, after carefully putting an aquascutum under you in case there are any nuns about. Look between the stalks of the wheat, and you see a great jungle of nettles, thistles, docks, poppies, willow-herb, bracken, briers, and goodness knows what. But it doesn't really matter, you know—they're not going to get past the threshing-machine. It's the bread that's important, not the field; the field is only there to produce the bread. It's heaven that's important, not earth; earth is only there to provide people for heaven.

The Gospel in Slow Motion

Or you can apply the parable rather differently; you can think of the crop as Christ's Church; that's what he meant, as I'm always telling you, when he talked about the kingdom of heaven. There *are* scandals in the Church, and if we don't come across big ones we all come across small ones; we come across priests who are very worldly, or so we think, and never seem to say their prayers if they can help it; we come across people who go to Communion every day and spend most of the rest of the day in uncharitable criticism of their neighbours. And we say to ourselves, "*Can* this be the true Church, when it produces such an awful lot of weeds?" But it is, you see; our Lord has told us that the Church is going to be like that. I remember long ago preaching a sermon in which I said that it was safer to leave your umbrella at the door of a Wesleyan chapel than at the door of a Catholic church; and the Wesleyans were awfully pleased about that, and have quoted me ever since. But they didn't quite get my point. My point was: Which is the Church that has cockle in it, like the Church our Lord talked about? And it isn't the Methodists.

But there's a third way in which you can apply this parable; and I want to suggest it to you today because it is the month of November, and we had a black Mass this morning, and we are all thinking about the Holy Souls. This mixture of cockle and wheat is to be found, not merely in the world we live in, not merely in the Church which has to be as universal as mankind, but in the life and character of the individual Christian, in you and me.

Think of the holiest person you know; even in that person your sharp eye has probably detected faults. She is, now and again, rather fussy and self-important; she is a little hard and unforgiving towards other people's sins; she is a little too fond of having her own way, or of attracting admiration—something of that kind. Cockle among the wheat, even there. And in your life and mine, what a mess the cockle makes! How much bad motives mix themselves up even with our good actions! We go to Mass and to Communion partly from love of God, partly because it would look bad if we didn't. We do a kind turn to somebody who has been nasty to us; partly from love of God, partly with a vague idea that we are scoring off her, showing her that we can behave more handsomely that she did. We give generously to some charity, partly from love of God but partly because it makes us feel rather fine fellows. Oh, it's all right; these good actions don't cease to be good actions simply because there are bad motives mixed up in them. My point is just that there nearly always are bad motives mixed up in them; just a spray or two of cockle among the wheat. Don't let's be depressed about it, but let's remember that it's there.

And let's remember this too—that it isn't always our good qualities people admire in this world; sometimes it's the bad ones. You say spiteful things, and that wins you the credit of being an amusing talker. You play the fool and waste a great deal of time and money, and people say, "How sporting she is!" You flatter people by agreeing with all the silly things they say, and approving of all the silly things they do; and they say, "How broad-minded she is!" It isn't always the good qualities in us that are the attractive qualities in us. That's why I reminded you just now that cockle is rather a jolly blue flower. It's pretty to look at, but it's not the thing the field is there for. If you point to a field of wheat and say to the farmer, "What lovely poppies you've got this year," he may not say much, but he'll think

The Gospel in Slow Motion

you an awful fool. And yet that is what you and I are doing all the time; admiring people for the wrong qualities, the ones that won't help them to get to heaven.

Well, here is a human soul, with this very mixed crop growing on it; what is God, the great Husbandman, going to do about it? Will he root out the bad qualities here and now, while it is still growing? Sometimes he does, but mostly in the lives of very holy people. God has a great weed-killer which he uses when he wants to clean up the field of a human soul; it is called suffering. In the lives of the Saints, you will see that weed-killer at work, eliminating all the bad motives. Everybody turns against them and speaks ill of them, so that their love of human praise, their fear of human disapproval, dies away. They are constantly losing their money and falling ill and being sent to prison, so that they don't serve God for the sake of anything they can get out of it in this world. Even their prayers, sometimes, get all dry and dull and distracted, so that they can find no pleasure in saying them; and they go on saying their prayers, not for the sake of any comfort they can derive from it, but just for the love of God. When that has been done; when suffering, the weed-killer, has done its work, God gets a hundred percent crop of wheat out of that field, or nearly a hundred percent crop.

But that is not his way with most of us. With most of us, he does what the farmer did in the parable; he waits till the harvest is gathered before he separates the wheat from the cockle, waits till we are dead and have been judged before he does anything about it. Then we go to Purgatory, and have the weeds in us burned away. When we say a Hail Mary for the Holy Souls, let's think of Purgatory as the bonfire which is burning up all the waste product there was in their lives; all in them that was of self, and not of God. Perhaps these qualities of theirs were attractive to us, perhaps we encouraged them by our admiration; encouraged So-and-so to be vain, encouraged So-and-so to be spiteful. Well, all the more reason why we should pray for them.

After this life, as in this life, God's weed-killer is suffering; the Holy Souls in Purgatory suffer. I don't know if you believe all those pious stories they tell you, about the priest who decided to put off saying a black Mass for some friend just dead, and then had a dream in which his friend appeared in the most horrible anguish, to show him what a dreadful thing he'd done. I shouldn't think that's true; or if it is I should think the priest had eaten something at dinner which didn't agree with him. We don't know anything really about how much the Holy Souls suffer, or the conditions under which they suffer. But we know that suffering comes into it, and therefore we ought to pray for them as we would pray for anybody on earth who was ill or having a bad time. And meanwhile, shall we sometimes think about our own lives, and all the waste-product there is in them; ask God if we can't be something rather more like a hundred percent wheat, before the time comes when death will reap us down, and the harvest of our lives will have to be winnowed, the little selfishnesses we so cling to here all winnowed away?

CHAPTER 7

St. Peter Looks Back

Indeed, you are engaged to this by the call of Christ; he suffered for our sakes, and left you his own example; you were to follow in his footsteps. He did no wrong, no treachery was found on his lips; he was ill spoken of, and spoke no evil in return, suffered, and did not threaten vengeance, gave himself up into the hands of injustice. So, on the cross, his own body took the weight of our sins; we were to become dead to our sins, and live for holiness; it was his wounds that healed you. Till then, you had been like sheep going astray; now, you have been brought back to him, your shepherd, who keeps watch over your souls. (1 PET. 2:21–25)

YOU HAVE ALL HEARD THAT EPISTLE READ AT MASS, BUT the chances are that most of you missed the point. The point of it is that St. Peter is talking to *slaves*. A good many of the early Christians were slaves, and they needed rather special directions when you wrote epistles. Because the slave in those days was completely at the disposal of his master, the master could beat him if he liked, kill him if he liked. There was one well-known Roman about that time, I forget who it was, who kept a pond with tame fish in it, and when he thought the fish were looking hungry he used to say,

RONALD KNOX

"Poor things," and kill a slave and throw him in for them to eat; which wasn't a very nice thing to do. And, curiously, if you look at the beginning of this first epistle of St. Peter, you find that he is writing to five different countries in Asia Minor, where the Turks live nowadays; and the name of one of those five was Cappadocia. If you pursue your researches further, and look up Cappadocia in a large Latin dictionary, you will find that slaves from Cappadocia were well-known for having enormous bodies but rather stupid intellects; which will give some of you a fellow-feeling for them. And St. Peter, who I think had preached in Cappadocia on his way to Rome, remembered those hulking great slaves who were always getting into trouble for leaving the bathwater running and one thing and another, so he thought he would put in a special bit in his epistle to cheer them up.

He says they must be submissive to their masters, not only to those who are kind and considerate, but to those who are hard to please. The Latin word used there really means "the ones who have bad digestions." It does a man credit (he goes on) when he bears undeserved ill-treatment, with the thought of God in his heart. If you do wrong and are punished for it, your patience is nothing to boast of; it is the patience of the innocent sufferer that wins credit in God's sight. That's a point of view we always rather tend to forget, don't we, when we are blamed for things that aren't our fault. We go about boiling with rage and wishing we could die suddenly in the night so that the mistress would be sorry for being so unkind, and all that sort of thing. But really, St. Peter says, it's rather splendid when you're blamed for something you haven't done, and can't make people believe you haven't done it. You've only got to

The Gospel in Slow Motion

take it patiently, and you win credit with God, who knows exactly what you have done and haven't done, and never attaches any blame where no blame is due. The longer you live, I think, the more you see that it doesn't really very much matter what people think. The only thing that matters is what God thinks, because what God thinks is always right.

Then, by way of comforting them over this situation of being blamed for things they hadn't done—which I should imagine was a pretty common experience with those Cappadocian slaves—he adds the bit you get at the beginning of this talk. It isn't really difficult, he says, to do what I'm telling you, because you've got a pattern, a model ready to hand; all the lines have been traced out for you, and you've only got to copy them. The word he uses means a heading in a copy-book. I expect you've all forgotten by now what it was like learning to write, because it was such a long time ago. But I can still remember learning to write, in a book with "Honesty is the best policy" or something of that kind all printed out at the top of the page, and lines underneath for me to make three copies of each sentence. The caption I remember best was, KEEP THE PEN POINTING LIKE A GUN OVER THE RIGHT SHOULDER; it seemed so odd of the copy-book to imagine that at the age of five you would know how to hold a gun and wouldn't know how to hold a pen. Well, St. Peter is saying here that all the slaves have got to do, when their masters have an attack of liver and start throwing the plates and saucers about, is to copy an example of patience which has already been traced for them. And of course what he is talking about is the patience of Jesus Christ, especially at the time of his Passion.

RONALD KNOX

It's perhaps well to remember that St. Peter is talking about something of which he was an eye-witness. St. Peter, if you come to think of it, knew something about slaves, if only because he had spent one night, one unforgettable night, in the servants' hall. You do not forget in a hurry the evening on which you denied your Master. And all this passage, I think, is simply a description of the way in which Jesus Christ behaved, and of the way in which Simon Peter behaved, on Maundy Thursday evening.

Our Lord did no wrong; no treachery was found on his lips. Left to themselves, the slaves St. Peter was writing to would tend to do just the opposite. They would do something wrong, would get into a bad temper, and break some rather valuable vase belonging to their masters out of spite; and then next morning they would lie about it; they'd say, "It wasn't me, it was him." It's very painful to have to mention such things to you, because of course it would never occur to *you* to do anything of the kind; but we are talking, remember, about the Cappadocian lower classes. Our Lord hadn't done anything wrong; but he stood silent before his judges in the council chamber; not defending himself, because he wanted to show a pattern to us others. They accused him, quite untruthfully, of all sorts of things; they said, for example, that he had threatened to destroy the temple; and he didn't say a word. It was only when they asked him, "Art thou the Christ, the Son of the living God?" that he broke silence and said, "Yes, I am." They taunted him, but he made no answer to their taunts; they struck him brutally, but he did not turn upon them and threaten vengeance. No; he gave himself up into the hands of injustice. There's an odd difference, there, between the Greek of the New Testament and the Latin. The Greek

The Gospel in Slow Motion

says he gave himself up to him who judges justly; the Latin says he gave himself up to him who judged unjustly. But of course the sense is the same in either case; it means that our Lord allowed his human accusers to say what they liked about him, to do what they liked to him, because he was content to leave the whole thing to God, who alone sees the truth, who alone never misjudges. He stood there passive, and nothing he could have done, nothing he could have said, would have been so effective a protest as his silence.

All that, remember, to St. Peter, who wrote his epistle, wasn't a picture he had to form with the imagination; he had *seen* it, memory brought it back to him, he had only to shut his eyes and it stood out before him, as vivid as if it had happened yesterday. And he, what had he been doing all the time? He'd been sitting over there in the firelight, lying, lying like mad. "Jesus of Nazareth? No, I don't think I ever heard the name…. From Galilee, you say? That's very odd, because it so happens I was never in Galilee in my life…. You say you recognize my face? You must have got me mixed up with somebody else…I never had anything to do with that man over there; I swear I've never set eyes on him till this evening!" All that comes back to St. Peter's mind as he sits there in the catacombs writing a letter to his slave friends in Cappadocia.

"Please, sir, it wasn't me, it was him"—what a familiar formula that is, when people are threatened with punishment; how familiar it must have been in the slave-compounds of St. Peter's time! The excuse may be true, or may be false; but, true or false, it lacks nobility. The general judgement of humanity, though it may pardon the liar, condemns the sneak. How rare, how refreshing to the ear is the contrary formula, "Please, sir, it wasn't him, it was me!" The unsuspected ready to suffer on behalf of the wrongfully accused; sometimes, in defiance of truth, the innocent ready to suffer instead of the guilty! All that will have crossed St. Peter's mind, thinking of his slave friends and their daily problems; and that suggests a fresh train of thought to him. That night, while he was cursing and swearing and denying all knowledge of Jesus of Nazareth, Jesus of Nazareth was suffering *instead of him*. Remember what happened in Gethsemani: a party of soldiers come out with a warrant to arrest Jesus of Nazareth; he submits, meekly enough, to their demands. Then, suddenly, in the darkness, one of his friends whips out a great sword and lays about him; the sword just catches one of the high priest's servants and cuts off his ear. Who is it? St. Peter, of course, only St. Peter could have made such a bad shot. Here is Peter, then, guilty of the one crime which no law ever pardons—violently interfering with the police in the execution of their duty. Peter, if anybody, ought to be marched off, and put on his trial for attempted murder. But what actually happens? Our Lord says to the soldiers, "If *I* am the man you are looking for, let these others go free." "Please, sir, it wasn't him, it was me…" Jesus of Nazareth goes off to face the charge of resisting the police; Peter has slipped away in the darkness.

Such are the inglorious memories that pass through the apostle's mind; and, naturally enough, they set him thinking about what our Lord's death really meant. Our Lord's death really meant that he took upon himself the punishment which our sins had deserved; *he* suffered here on earth to let *us* off our sufferings in eternity. And St. Peter tells the Cappadocian slaves about that, in language which slaves can understand. "His own body took the weight of our sins";

The Gospel in Slow Motion

there is nothing those slaves do not know about carrying heavy burdens; they are doing it all the time. And in what circumstances? On a cross. Crucifixion was the punishment regularly inflicted on slaves when they were condemned to death; these Cappadocians had seen it happen often enough. "It was his wounds that healed you"—strictly speaking, his scars, the great livid bruises left by the lash on human shoulders. That was a quotation from the prophet Isaias; St. Peter didn't invent it, but he saw that it was the right quotation for the people he was talking to—most of them had such scars on their backs, only partly healed. And he tells them to think of the whipping their sins had deserved in eternity, and how the innocent shoulders of Jesus of Nazareth intercepted those cruel blows, took the marks of them instead. Our Lord didn't suffer *merely* so as to set us an example of the spirit in which we ought to suffer. He suffered for our sins, the innocent on behalf of the guilty. "It wasn't him, it was me" is the characteristic protest of the Crucified.

And then, I think, St. Peter's mind travels back a little further, and he remembers how his denial of our Lord had been prophesied beforehand by our Lord himself. What were the words our Lord used when he told his apostles beforehand what a poor figure they were going to cut? Why, these: "Tonight you will all lose courage over me; for so it has been written, I will smite the shepherd, and the sheep of his flock will be scattered. But I will go on before you, when I have risen from the dead." That's a picture familiar to most of us. When a party of sheep from the lower ground get out and start wandering down the drive, how idiotic and pointless their motions look! Some of them, apparently, determined to find a back way into the tennis-court, others starting out for a day's shopping in Bridgnorth. That foolish want, of purpose and of leadership the apostles showed when our Lord was arrested; and St. Peter remembers it with peculiar vividness, because after all it was he who ought to have rallied them, and he did nothing of the kind. They just huddled away in the Cenacle, like sheep under a hedge, with no idea what they were going to do next. St. Peter remembers it with peculiar vividness, because a few days later, when our Lord had risen and gone on before them, he, the shepherd, at the head of his flock, into Galilee, the mention of shepherding had come into the conversation again. "Simon, son of John, lovest thou me? Feed my lambs, feed my shearlings, feed my sheep…." The bad shepherd had been turned into a good shepherd, that day on the hillside in Galilee.

Probably some of the slaves St. Peter was writing to spent their time looking after their masters' flocks; and so, before he finishes this short message of his which is specially addressed to them, he brings in that metaphor too, the metaphor his Divine Master was so fond of. "Till then, you had been like sheep going astray; now, you have been brought back to him, your shepherd, who keeps watch over your souls." How comfortably that rounds off today's epistle! The good shepherd has given his life for his sheep, and now he watches over them to keep them from harm; he is the bishop of their souls, that is the strict meaning of the phrase St. Peter uses; he, the chief of bishops on earth, likes to remember and to remind his converts that they have a greater Bishop in heaven. One of the chief duties of a bishop, St. Paul tells us, is to be a pattern to his flock; and the Bishop of our souls has left a pattern for us, his flock, to follow. He has shown us how to take the world's judgements with complete indifference, committing our cause to the justice of our Father in heaven; how to suffer, if need be, for the faults of others, glad, if the occasion arises, to imitate the example of that unique Victim, who gave his life for us all.

CHAPTER 9

The Devil Goes House-Hunting

He had just cast out a devil, which was dumb; and no sooner had the devil gone out than the dumb man found speech. The multitudes were filled with amazement; but some of them said, It is through Beelzebub, the prince of the devils, that he casts the devils out, while others, to put him to the test, would have him show a sign out of heaven. But he could read their thoughts, and said to them, No kingdom can be at war with itself without being brought to desolation, one house falling upon another. And how do you suppose that Satan's kingdom can stand firm if he is at war with himself, that you should accuse me of casting out devils through Beelzebub? Again, if it is through Beelzebub that I cast out devils, by what means do your own sons cast them out? It is for these, then, to pronounce judgement on you. But if, when I cast out devils, I do it through God's power, then it must be that the kingdom of God has suddenly appeared among you. When a strong man, fully armed, mounts guard over his own palace, his goods are left in peace; but when a man comes who is stronger still, he will take away all the armour that gave him confidence, and divide among others the spoils he has won. He who is not with me, is against me; he who does not gather his store with me, scatters it abroad. The unclean spirit which has possessed a man and

RONALD KNOX

then goes out of him, walks about the desert looking for a resting-place, and finds none; and it says, I will go back to my own dwelling, from which I came out. And it comes back, to find that dwelling swept out, and neatly set in order. Thereupon, it goes away and brings in seven other spirits more wicked than itself to bear it company, and together they enter in and settle down there; till the last state of that man is worse than the first. When he spoke thus, a woman in the multitude said to him aloud, Blessed is the womb that bore thee, the breast which thou hast sucked. And he answered, Shall we not say, Blessed are those who hear the word of God, and keep it? (LUKE 11:14–28)

THIS IS ONE OF THOSE FEW GOSPELS—THE UNJUST STEWARD is another—which make everybody go away from church asking, "What on earth was all that about?" Yet the lesson of it is enormously important, and specially important for us Catholics, so it's a pity if we go away thinking it doesn't mean anything. The part of the gospel I want to preach about is the part about the evil spirit going out of the man and coming back again. Our Lord starts, you will remember, by saying how silly it is of the Pharisees to imagine that he only manages to cast out devils because he is possessed by a devil himself; is it likely, he asks, that Satan should want to queer his own pitch? And then he goes on to draw the moral, for fear they shouldn't see it. When a strong man armed keeps his house, his goods are at peace; when a tyrant rules, there are no rows among the population, because they know it would mean concentration camps for them if they made any rows. If the strong man is turned out, it means that somebody else has come along from outside; a foreign power which has more tanks and more aeroplanes than the tyrant has; humanly speaking, the chances are enormously against the tyrant being turned out anyhow else. Well then, our Lord says, what is happening here? The devil, we all know, is much stronger than men; and for centuries past he has had such a lot to say in human affairs that you may practically say he controls the world. And if now all over Judaea, all over Galilee, you find devils being driven out from the unfortunate people whom they possessed, what does it mean? It can only mean that someone who is stronger than the devil has come along, and is stripping him of his spoils.

And when you can see with your own eyes that I am stronger than the devil, can't you make a guess who I am?

So far, it's all plain sailing; then we get to this difficult passage I want to talk about. And I suppose the first impression we get is that it's rather odd of our Lord, who generally stuck to plain everyday subjects to illustrate his teaching, like a shepherd losing his sheep or a king going out to war or a butler putting new wine into old bottles, should suddenly, on this one occasion, have given us a little disquisition on the natural history (or perhaps we should call it the preternatural history) of evil spirits. But I don't think, you know, that he really meant to tell us very much about that. I think he put his parable in that particular form because the Pharisees had raised the subject of devils generally; so it made a good starting-place. And, as Maldonatus points out (Maldonatus is one of the few commentators on the Bible who are worth looking at; he was a Jesuit who lived four hundred years ago, but he is very fresh reading), our Lord is really attributing to the evil spirit the habits of a man, and the circumstances of a man; so we mustn't expect to learn a great deal about the ways or the outlook of devils from this passage.

RONALD KNOX

Well, let us look at our picture first of all, without bothering yet about the interpretation. It isn't, clearly, meant to be the kind of thing that often happens, like the sower going out to sow. It is the kind of thing that might occasionally happen, like the butler who was fool enough to put new wine, still unfermented, into old skin bottles, which of course burst. This is the sort of thing that might happen, our Lord says, if you're not careful. And it doesn't really matter much whether the hero of the story is a devil, or a man, or a beast for that matter. If we found that a man-eating tiger had made its lair in the wood by the Shore Pool, and succeeded in making it go away, we shouldn't leave the lair just as it was, for fear the tiger should come back. We should put pieces of broken bottles in it and all the things which make the sort of smells tigers don't like, if we could find out what those are—turpentine is rather good for rats. And in the same way if it were a man that we had evicted; you mustn't read this story of the evil spirit going round house-hunting, and think of his "house" as a maisonnette at Golders Green. No, think of a brigand up in the hills somewhere, hunted out at last by the police but not caught; if the police had any sense they wouldn't leave his cave or disused factory or whatever it was he lived in just as it was, or he might be tempted to come back there; they would block up the cave or blow up the factory, so that he would go off and rob somebody else instead. Still less, if they had any sense, would they do up the cave or the disused factory and put a respectable citizen in to live there. The brigand would come back one fine afternoon with a party of friends, and say, "I like this; it's rather classy"; and the new tenants would find it occupied when they got back from the matinee. That, our Lord says, rather mysteriously, is what the evil spirit will do if you are not careful. He will come back to the soul he haunted once, and make himself more at home there than ever.

What I read to you was St. Luke's account. If you look up the passage in the twelfth chapter of St. Matthew you will find it word for word the same—I doubt if there is any passage where two evangelists are so closely agreed about the actual words our Lord used—but there is a postscript which St. Luke has left out. "So shall it be," our Lord adds, "with this evil generation." It is a parable, you see, not just a story; and like most of his parables it refers in the first instance not to individuals, to your soul or mine, but to a whole people—the guilty people of the Jews who did not receive our Lord when he came to them, would not listen when he preached to them, hung him on a cross when they could bear his rebukes no longer. Somehow they are in the position of the soul, once possessed, which has now been exorcized; or, if you will, of the village that has got rid of its brigand and wants him to transfer his activities elsewhere. The home he knows is the home he will turn back to when he grows tired of house-hunting; and if he comes back, he must not find it swept and garnished, ready for his tenancy. What are we to make of all that? What warning is our Lord conveying to the men of his own age?

St. Chrysostom had rather an ingenious theory to account for it. He said that our Lord was thinking, as he so often did think, about the destruction of Jerusalem by the Roman armies, forty years after his death. The evil spirit in the parable represents those world-conquerors who were for ever annexing Palestine to their empires because it held such a key position in the ancient world—holds a key position, for that matter, in the modern world still. You have escaped, our Lord says to the Jews, from the Babylonian conquerors of five hundred years back, from the Seleucid conquerors of two hundred years back; those empires have disappeared, and their influence has been exorcized, you think, for ever. But, in forty years from now, the evil spirit will come back, this time in more formidable force than ever, the Romans will destroy Jerusalem much more thoroughly than Nabuchodonosor ever did, much more thoroughly than Antiochus Epiphanes ever did. And the last state of the Jewish people will be worse than the first. Well, I could preach you a very topical sermon about all that; because really nowadays when you talk about a country being liberated it means taking it away from somebody and giving it to somebody else. But I don't think St. Chrysostom's theory is right. If you like to adopt that interpretation, you have a very respectable doctor of the Church to quote for it. But I don't think our Lord was talking about politics, or about the material troubles that were to come upon the Jewish people, just here. I think he was talking about the state of their souls. The point is, I think, that the man who has been exorcized and so has got rid of a devil has received an enormous spiritual favour. And so had the Jews received enormous spiritual favours. They had been given the ten commandments, they had been taught that there was only one God, their prophets had educated them to the hope of a Messiah. Everywhere else people worshipping idols, people making beasts of themselves, people killing one another; Palestine, where the Jews lived, the one bright spot, you would say, in a horrible world; the one place where the devil seemed to have been driven out. And so he had, in a fashion. The trouble was that he got bored

The Gospel in Slow Motion

with trying to lead the Gentiles into sin; it was too easy. He was like the house-hunter wandering about in waterless places, seeking rest and finding none. The Gentiles were too easy a prey; it seemed hardly sporting to put temptations in *their* way. So he thought he would come back to the place from which he had been driven out: to Palestine. And when he came, he found it swept and garnished.

That, obviously, is the whole point of the parable, and the whole nub of the difficulty. Why is it that our Lord compares the state of the man who has been set free from an evil spirit, or the state of the Jews in his own day, to that of a house which is all neat and tidy, with all the cushions quite straight on the chairs, and a strong smell of beeswax coming from the floors? That is obviously what it means; we don't use the word "garnish" nowadays except to describe the action of a cook in putting bits of parsley round the cold meat, merely to make the cold meat look less cold, not because parsley is good to eat—at least, I never want to eat parsley. The idea, anyhow, is that of a house in almost irritatingly spick and span order. At first sight, it seems rather bad luck on the lay sisters, don't you think, that our Lord seems to disapprove of having everything scrubbed and polished, when they spend almost their whole lives scrubbing and polishing? Well, let us comfort them by pointing out that our Lord doesn't say beeswax is a bad thing in itself. All he says is that finding the front-doorstep so carefully washed and all the antimacassars so straight was a temptation to the devil to come back. And what he means, surely, is that the very virtues of the Jews were a danger to them. Their terribly negative virtues; *not* doing any work on the sabbath day, *not* eating things cooked with the blood in them, *not* sitting down to eat with Gentiles; their terribly pompous virtues, praying and fasting and giving alms in a very obvious way, so as to make everybody say, "Gosh, what pious people"; their terribly niggling virtues, taking tithe of mint and anise and cumin and always trying to see how little they could do for God and still qualify as God-fearing people—all that gave the devil his chance. It was like a house with all the furniture covered in dust-sheets, that hasn't been lived in for months. The Jewish soul had a large notice up outside it saying TO LET, and the devil said, "Oh, very well, let's go back to the old stand." In a sense, it wasn't because they were so wicked that the Jews crucified our Lord. It was because they were so good, so negatively, so pompously, so nigglingly good.

On all that, Maldonatus has a curious comment which I want to leave with you, because, as I say, I think this parable of our Lord's is so frightfully important. Maldonatus says, "There are no worse Catholics than those who were at one time very religious, but couldn't stick to what they had got." On paper, you see, it's perfectly possible to get to heaven by being negatively good, not crashing the ten commandments, not *not* going to Mass; by being pompously good, designing your whole life so that it shall be a scolding for other people; by being nigglingly good, always seeing how near the wind you can sail by just keeping clear of mortal sin, always balancing your score of venial sins against your score of indulgences. But I wonder how many people *really* get to heaven like that? Some of you, perhaps, will; some of you haven't got the temperaments for it. It must be real love of God, not just playing for safety; real love of your neighbour, not just a cold regard for your neighbour's rights, if your religion is going to stand the strain later on. If he finds you trying to lounge through the world negatively, pompously, nigglingly good, the devil will look at your soul and say, "Just the place for me! Just look at those lobelias in the borders, just look how well the door-handle is polished! I must say, I do like a place that has been kept tidy!" And the last state of that woman will be worse than the first; a Catholic who has gone wrong does so much more harm in the world than a Protestant who has never gone right.

Well, don't write home and say, "Monsignor Knox preached us a sermon against being good," or I shall get into trouble. I only mean, don't be satisfied with yourself when you find there isn't much to mention on Saturday evening, only the time you made a face when the lay mistress wasn't looking, and the time you said you'd brushed your teeth when you hadn't. Don't be satisfied if you find you aren't really wanting to love God better, if you find that you aren't sometimes wanting to *do* things because of him, if you find it doesn't cost you any effort much being the kind of Catholic you are. Always, if you are to be safe, your head must be pointing upstream. Always your justice must be exceeding the justice of the scribes and Pharisees; you must be loving people, not just not hating them; giving things away, not just being honest; telling the truth, not just not telling lies. Your soul must be a house so fully tenanted with the love of God, that when the devil comes house-hunting and looks for the TO LET notice, he finds a strip of paper pasted across it inscribed with the single word SOLD.

CHAPTER 10

The Test

And now Jesus was led by the Spirit away into the wilderness, to be tempted there by the devil. Forty days and forty nights he spent fasting, and at the end of them was hungry. Then the tempter approached, and said to him, If thou art the Son of God, bid these stones turn into loaves of bread. He answered, It is written, Man cannot live by bread only; there is life for him in all the words which proceed from the mouth of God. Next, the devil took him into the holy city, and there set him down on the pinnacle of the temple, saying to him, If thou art the Son of God, cast thyself down to earth; for it is written, He has given charge to his angels concerning thee, and they will hold thee up with their hands, lest thou shouldst chance to trip on a stone. Jesus said to him, But it is further written, Thou shalt not put the Lord thy God to the proof. Once more, the devil took him to the top of an exceedingly high mountain, from which he showed him all the kingdoms of the world and the glory of them, and said, I will give thee all these if thou wilt fall down and worship me. Then Jesus said to him, Away with thee, Satan; it is written, Thou shalt worship the Lord thy God, and serve none but him. Then the devil left him alone; and thereupon angels came and ministered to him. (MATT. 4:1–11)

RONALD KNOX

THIS BEING THE FIRST SUNDAY OF LENT, I THOUGHT I should look for something appropriate in the epistle or gospel of the day. But when you come to look into it, you find that today's epistle has only two sentences about Lent, and those are the first two sentences. The rest of it is advice to clergymen about how they ought to behave, considering the fact that they are ambassadors of Christ. *You* might preach *me* a very telling sermon about that, knowing my faults as you do, and give me a really useful scolding. But *I* can't preach *you* a very useful sermon about it, because you aren't clergymen and aren't going to be. So I thought I would preach to you about the Gospel, about our Lord's Temptation, instead.

As we all know, Lent is the time when we go into training for the spiritual conflict. And we start it by taking a good look at our Lord, as he stood there out in the wilderness, waiting to be tempted by the devil. You all know the sort of books that give you photographs of star tennis-players, for example, in all sorts of odd attitudes which look as if they had got twisted up into a knot somewhere in midair. And I dare say some of you have tried to practise putting yourselves into those odd attitudes by way of improving your own game. Well, that's what this gospel for the first Sunday of Lent is about. It shows you our Lord, the great Hero we are all out to imitate, in certain characteristic poses or poises which he had to adopt in order to resist the temptations of the devil. When a person's going to box, or to wrestle, he starts from the first in a defensive attitude, all on his toes, all his muscles tense, all his nerves on the alert. And that, of course, is how you and I ought to meet the devil. Instead of which, he nearly always finds us slumped up anyhow like a bag of potatoes when it's only half full, and of course he has an uncommonly easy time with us.

I'm not going to talk to you about fasting, because that would take up too much time; we mustn't have an extra-long sermon today, while you are all sitting there giving one another colds. Our Lord had been fasting (there's no way of telling whether that means he had eaten nothing, or that he'd eaten very little) for forty days. Only don't imagine that fasting, or doing without things which you like, is necessarily going to preserve you from temptation. On the contrary, going without food, for instance, is apt to bring with it the temptation to be snappy and short-tempered. And here, you see, the fact that our Lord had been fasting was a good opportunity for the devil. He wanted to find out whether our Lord was the Son of God or just an ordinary man. And he said to himself, "If this is just an ordinary man, after forty days of fasting he will be ravenous for food; if he's the Son of God, that sort of thing doesn't matter to him. We'll see what he makes of it if I suggest food." Note that the devil always tries to seize upon what is our weak point at the moment; fend him off, until the mood of the present moment has passed, and he will be much easier to deal with. Note also that the devil likes to appeal to us through the imagination. He points to the round, flat stones that are lying about in the desert, and says to our Lord: "Funny-looking stones; almost like loaves of bread, aren't they? Pity they aren't loaves of bread, eh? Look here, if you are the Son of God, why not turn them into loaves?" Learn to keep your eyes guarded so that they are not accustomed to the sight of evil, if you want to keep evil away from the stronghold of your imagination.

RONALD KNOX

Well, at this point you probably want to raise an objection. "Would it have been sinful," you say, "for our Lord to have turned the stones into bread and eaten them, and, if so, why?" Of course, if you are going to raise objections like that, we shan't get on nearly so fast with the sermon. I think the simplest way to put it is this: If some shepherd had left the remains of his luncheon lying about, and the devil had pointed to them and said, "You are hungry, why not have something to eat?" then there could have been no sin, no imperfection even, *as far as we know*, in yielding to the suggestion. But it wasn't that; our Lord was entrusted with miraculous powers for the benefit of other people. He had the power to create bread in the wilderness, to be used, as he used it later on, when his followers were hungry. But these powers were not given to him for his own benefit; and to have used them to satisfy his own hunger would have been a misuse of the powers given him. Sin, for you and me, consists in using our natural powers sinfully, for purposes for which they were not meant. And our Lord would have been doing that with the supernatural powers entrusted to him; so it would have been wrong. Meanwhile if he *had* done that, the devil would have found out the answer to his question. He would have known that our Lord, if he behaved like that, was not the Son of God, he was only an ordinary man.

What is our Lord's answer? At first sight, it looks rather off the point. It's true, man doesn't live by bread alone; a human being who lives only for eating and drinking is an unpleasant object; what we mostly call a pig. But one has to eat in order to keep alive; life consists partly in eating. So was our Lord's answer really an answer? Wasn't he dodging the point? The answer to that is that he *was* dodging the point; he was saying, in effect, "Let's talk about something else. Here have I been for forty days in conversation with my heavenly Father; and I've been living so much *in* that conversation and *for* that conversation, that I'd quite forgotten to take my meals—till *you* came and interrupted." It's really a polite way of saying, "Go away." And what you've got to note there, is that that is commonly the best way of dealing with the devil's suggestions—to change the subject. Not to argue with him, not to try and weigh up the rights and wrongs of his suggestion, but to change the subject. If you're being tempted, for example, to brood over an injury, don't sit there biting your pocket-handkerchief and saying, "I won't be angry with Mary Jane! Please, Lord, help me to forget what a beast Mary Jane has been." Go and clean out your rabbit-hutch. Still more important, change the subject when conversation is beginning to get uncharitable. Don't *argue* with your temptations.

It's time we got on to the second one. The devil takes our Lord—bodily, why not? Far less odd that Satan should have the power of conveying our Lord's body about, than that he should have had the power of making suggestions to his mind—takes our Lord and puts him down on the pinnacle of the temple. You know how standing on a high place like that always makes one wonder what it would be like if one fell off. Our Lord knew that if he fell off, Divine Providence wouldn't allow him to be killed; he had a work to do, a mission to fulfil. And the devil uses that knowledge of his to suggest a fresh temptation. "Look at all those people down below, crawling there like ants! Suppose you jumped off, instead of falling off, and all those hundreds of human faces looked upwards, and saw you floating through the air, instead of falling to your death! Because

87

of course you *would* float through the air; the angels would *have* to bear you up in their hands—that is, *if* you are the Son of God."

You see what's passing through the devil's mind there, don't you? He still isn't certain himself whether our Lord is the Son of God or not; and, finding that his first suggestion has been dodged like that, he begins to think our Lord himself isn't quite certain, either. So he suggests a new test, which our Lord will certainly have to refuse if he is not the Son of God, and knows that he isn't. But our Lord's answer leaves him in the dark. "Thou shalt not tempt the Lord thy God." I hope none of you are so silly as to imagine that means, "You, Satan, ought not to be tempting me, who am the Lord your God." Of course, it doesn't mean that; it means, "I, Jesus of Nazareth, must not make trial of the Lord my God, must not put the Lord my God to the proof. I must not plunge myself unnecessarily into danger, and then challenge him to let me perish if he has the heart to. I must not *tempt Providence*." Well, of course, the devil doesn't tempt you and me to throw ourselves down over precipices; he doesn't waste his time tempting people to do things which have no sort of attraction for them. But he does tempt us, sometimes, to take *spiritual* risks which are far graver risks (if we could only realize it) than a hundred-foot drop. He tempts us to make our friends in dangerous company, to soak our minds in dangerous reading, to allow ourselves liberties where love and friendship are concerned, and say to ourselves, "Oh, that'll be all right. After all, one must have a reasonable confidence in Divine Providence. God won't let me down; *he* knows I don't mean any harm." That is tempting God; that is presuming on grace. The rule of Divine Providence is that God won't force you into any position of spiritual danger without offering you the grace that will see you through. He doesn't undertake to offer you the grace which will see you through if you run your head into a noose, if you deliberately neglect ordinary prudence. That, I hope, is evident to all of us; I hope all of you will remember it later on.

And there's the third temptation; the top of the high mountain—I think it was Carmel. From Carmel you looked down on the great plain of Esdraelon, where the fate of empires had so often been decided—was so often to be decided again. That, if you looked landwards; and if you looked seawards, your eye swept the Mediterranean, and saw the great ships pass by carrying corn from Egypt to imperial Rome. It made you think, either way, of empires and of worldly greatness. By now, I think, Satan had come to the conclusion, provisionally, that our Lord *wasn't* the Son of God; would he have flunked that last test if he had been? Let us proceed, then, on the supposition that he is Man, just an ordinary man—the third temptation, you will notice, doesn't begin like the other two with the words, "If thou be the Son of God." If this is an ordinary man, and I offer him all the kingdoms of the world, in return for doing homage to me as the legitimate owner of them, surely he must fall for it? For a man with big ideas like that, who wants to convert the whole world, it would be hardly human not to…. But once more our Lord declines the test. He doesn't say, "I'm the Son of God, and therefore your offer is no use to me"; nor does he accept the offer. He answers that whether he is the Son of God or no, he is the servant of God, and cannot exchange that service.

All the kingdoms of the world—one might take that opportunity to preach against Hitler or Stalin. But Hitler and Stalin aren't here, and I always think it's a pity to scold people who aren't there when you're preaching a sermon. *You* almost certainly won't be offered all the kingdoms of the world. But it is quite possible that, later on, you *will* be offered worldly prosperity at the price of going against your conscience; a suitable marriage, perhaps, and a comfortable home, if there are such things as comfortable homes left by the time you are grown up, or a good job, perhaps—if you will betray your conscience, if you will fall down and worship the devil. God grant that, if that happens, the devil may find you ready squared up to meet the temptation, however sudden it may be; and not slumped up like a half-full bag of potatoes, asking for trouble.

CHAPTER II

The Magi and the Centurion

A great multitude followed him when he had come down from the mountain; and now, a leper came and knelt before him, and said, Lord, if it be thy will, thou hast power to make me clean. Jesus held out his hand and touched him, and said, It is my will; be thou made clean. Whereupon his leprosy was immediately cleansed. Then Jesus said, Be sure thou dost not tell any man of it; rather go and show thyself to the priest, and offer the gift which Moses ordained, to make the truth known to them.

As he entered Capharnaum, a centurion came to him, asking for his aid; Lord, he said, I have a servant lying sick at my house, cruelly tormented with the palsy. Jesus said to him, I will come and heal him. But the centurion answered, Lord, I am not worthy to receive thee under my roof; my servant will be healed if thou wilt only speak a word of command. I, too, know what it is to obey authority; I have soldiers under me, and I say, Go, to one man, and he goes, or, Come, to another, and he comes, or, Do this, to my servant, and he does it. When he heard that, Jesus said to his followers in amazement, Believe me, I have not found faith like this, even in Israel. And this I tell you, that there are many who will come from the east and from the west, and will take their places in the kingdom of God with Abraham and Isaac and Jacob, while that kingdom's

RONALD KNOX

own sons are cast into the darkness without, where there will be weeping, and gnashing of teeth. And to the centurion Jesus said, Go then; let it be done to thee as thy faith foretold. And at that hour his servant was healed. (MATT. 8:1–13)

I ALWAYS LIKE TO THINK OF ONE SMALL DETAIL ABOUT THE Nativity. I take it that the Wise Men slept at the inn, which was the same inn where there was no room for our Lady and St. Joseph. And it must have made the innkeeper feel pretty small when he found that these rich and important people had come to see the party in the stable. We have no evidence, of course, that they were really kings, any more than that one of them was black; but they would be rich and important people with luggage that took a lot of carrying upstairs, and probably very ornamental hats, and the inn-keeper would be impressed; he must have felt very small when he found that they had come from the ends of the earth to see the child whose father and mother were turned out, the other day, in the snow.

I'm afraid that is rather like inn-keepers all the world over. He liked to have scientific gentlemen from foreign parts staying in his hotel; but when it came to a poor working-man ringing the bell late at night, and all the trouble it would mean, he very naturally said, "No, you go along; it's not for you to come under my roof," "It's not for you to come under my roof"—that was how the king of the Jews was received by the Jews themselves. He came to his own, and his own treated him as a stranger. And meanwhile these Gentiles from the remote east had come all the way to find him. That is of course the chief point of the Epiphany.

The Gospel in Slow Motion

Years passed by, and St. Joseph died his happy death, and our Lord began his ministry up in Galilee. He didn't go on living at Nazareth; he had settled by now at Capharnaum, not far off. The gospels are always mysteriously saying, "when he had come into the house," or something like that, and making us want to ask "What house?" Well, we can't be certain, but I suppose it was his house. Or rather, since the Son of Man had nowhere to lay his head, I suppose it was the house that belonged to his family; that is, to our Blessed Lady. And I like to think of her standing there in Capharnaum and listening to her Son preaching, and watching him do miracles. Perhaps she was standing there one day when an unusual figure appeared among the queue of people that was surging up to ask for his aid—a centurion in the uniform of the Roman army. A centurion, remember, was a non-commissioned officer, a sergeant, perhaps, quartered in Galilee and not very popular with the Galileans, who didn't like to be reminded that they were a subject country. I shouldn't think he got a very good place in the queue.

And what a queue! "Master, my daughter is lying at the point of death" ... "Master, my son is grievously vexed with a devil" ... "Have mercy on me, thou son of David; Lord, that I may see!" And everybody at once saying, "Do *come*, Lord, come *quick*; please *come*." And here is this foreign sergeant, in his unpopular uniform; what is *his* story going to be? He has a servant, perhaps a native Syrian boy, who started a twitch the other day, and now he is shaking all over; and the doctors say it is a palsy and they don't think there is anything they can do about it. Well, the morning wears on, and at last the centurion gets his chance. He stands to attention, and puts his case in the briefest possible language, "I have a servant at my house, cruelly tormented with the palsy." He doesn't say, "Come, please come at once," like the others. He just says what is the matter; and our Lord, who liked people to get to the point, looks at him gratefully. "I will come and heal him"—that was the last thing the centurion expected to hear. "Oh no, sir, I couldn't ask you to do that; I live in quite a small way, and my house isn't fit for the likes of you—it's not for you to come under my roof. I know what it is to be part of a military machine, being ordered about and ordering other people about; telling this man to go and he goes, this man to come and he comes, and my poor servant, as long as he kept his health, running and doing errands for me all the time. The way I look at it is, you're a superior officer, a sort of General Officer in Command; and these are your headquarters. Well, the General doesn't go into the front line; he stays at headquarters and gives his orders from there. That's all I want you to do; give the word of command, and my servant will get well quick enough. No need for *you* to put yourself to the trouble of coming round to *my* place."

Do you know how sometimes you have the sudden feeling that all this has happened before? You were in a room just like this, and standing just here, and somebody made exactly the same remark that has been made just now by the person you are talking to—you could have told him what he was going to say before he opened his lips. Did it happen before in real life, or was it in a dream? Or is there some subtler explanation? That was the feeling our Lady got, I expect, when she stood there listening to the centurion. "It's not for you to come under my roof"—where was it, when was it, that she heard those words before? And then the scene comes back to her—the inn-keeper at Bethlehem, long ago, and the very different tone of voice in which he said, "It's not for *you* to come under *my* roof."

Our Lord knew what people were thinking all around him, and I expect he knew his Blessed Mother's mind pretty well. He stands astonished at the faith of the centurion; this Gentile who only asks him to say a word of command while everybody else is shouting, "Come, please come!" ... "I haven't found such faith," he says, "even among my own people of Israel." And then he looks at his Mother, and smiles, as he thinks of the Wise Men from the east who came to his cradle, and were put up at the inn where there was no room to receive the King of Angels. And he goes on, "There are many who will come from the east and from the west, and will take their places in the Kingdom of God with Abraham and Isaac and Jacob, while that kingdom's own sons are cast into the darkness without."

From the east and from the west—those wise men came from the east, from the mysterious countries that know all about magic, and understand the motions of the stars; they stood there talking a mysterious language, offering mysterious gifts, going off mysteriously into the night; it was all very wonderful, but almost frightening; the whole thing seemed like a dream. And now, this man from the west, this Roman soldier, how different! He may have come from farther west than Italy; he may have come from Gaul or Spain. But the great thing about him is that he is so splendidly practical; has the great military tradition of Rome so deeply rooted in his outlook. *You* stand here and do this, *you* go there and do that; and you—ah, you are my superior officer. You don't need to go here or there; you give the word of command, and your orders are obeyed.

RONALD KNOX

Nothing mysterious about this man; he is all plain common sense; he sees the supernatural world marked out like a manual of military discipline.

From the east and from the west—it takes all sorts to make a Church. You will sometimes hear people describe the Christian religion as an eastern religion; it isn't anything of the sort. Sometimes it is just the other way round, people will tell you: "Ah, of course you don't understand the way these Buddhists look at things, the way these Brahmins look at things; you are a westerner, and you don't understand the eastern mind." But that isn't true either. Our Lord, when he came to earth, deliberately chose Palestine as the country he was going to be born in. Bethlehem is almost exactly the same distance west of London as it is east of Bombay, almost exactly the same distance west of New York as it is east of Tokyo. And the religion which our Lord came to found was meant to attract wise men from the east, but it was also meant to attract fools from the west, like you and me. It has mystery, like the eastern religions; the long silences at Mass, the shut doors of the tabernacle, the singing of Latin words which you don't understand; all that gives distance and majesty to the Christian cult. And at the same time it is full of the practical common sense on which we western people pride ourselves; the Penny Catechism is as businesslike, in its way, as the multiplication table. The three kings making their salaams in the darkness of the stable, and the centurion clicking his heels and saluting in broad daylight on the seafront at Capharnaum—it's all part of the same Church.

Yes, it's very comforting to think of those people coming from the east and the west and taking their places with Abraham and

The Gospel in Slow Motion

Isaac and Jacob; the word suggests taking places at table, by the way. Our Lord is using, you see, a nice homely metaphor; he represents the kingdom of heaven, his Church, in terms of a family meal. There is Abraham, sitting up at the end of the table, carving, and there is Isaac and Jacob and the whole family complete… at least, unfortunately, it isn't complete. There are Abraham and Isaac and Jacob, and there are Melchior and Caspar and Balthasar, and there is the centurion lifting his glass and saying, "Well, here's health." But where is the inn-keeper, who said there was no room for our Lady and St. Joseph in the inn? Where are all those Jews of our Lord's time, who ought to have known exactly what was happening, and didn't? The children of the kingdom will be cast into the exterior darkness; do you see them there, flattening their noses against the window-pane, and wishing they could even *smell* the turkey and plum-pudding? That is the nice homely metaphor in which our Lord puts the terrible truth, "He came unto his own, and his own did not receive him." These Gentiles did the best they could with what they had got. These wise men out in the east didn't know anything about the God of Israel, but they kept on watching the stars. And although it's a pretty silly business watching the stars, and you shouldn't pay any attention to the paragraphs in the cheap papers about what the stars foretell, God did arrange just that once that the stars should tell what was happening, and the wise men got on their camels straight away. The centurion wasn't an expert in theology, but he knew a little about military discipline, and that little was enough to show him the right way of addressing our Lord when he wanted to get his servant healed. But so many of the Jews, who'd been told exactly what to expect and exactly when to expect it, simply didn't know what was happening when our Lord came. And the party had to be made up without them.

So, you see, this text about people coming from the east and the west isn't only a comforting text, to make us more keen on contributing to the black babies; it's also a warning text, telling us Catholics to be very careful, because God has given us so many opportunities, so many graces, and we have got to rise to those opportunities, to correspond with those graces. Otherwise, when it comes to the general judgement, the party will have to be made up without us. How often it happens, doesn't it, that we meet Protestants, and even people with no religion to speak of, who can give us points and a beating when it comes to kindness, and unselfishness, and honesty, and so on! When that happens, we oughtn't to say, "Well, I can't see much point in the Christian religion if it doesn't make me as fine a person as So-and-so!" We ought to say, "How dreadful, that with all the start God has given me, I should still be so hopelessly behind!" It oughtn't to make us feel despairing; it ought to make us feel humble.

And more especially, we ought to feel humble about it when we go to Communion, and think about the little use we have made of the graces given us so far. The priest uses the centurion's words, doesn't he, with a slight difference; "Lord, I am not worthy that thou shouldst come under my roof, but speak the word only, and my soul shall be healed." Your soul, all at sixes and sevens, like the centurion's house, is not fit to be seen by visitors. I dare say some of you have had a nightmare before now, only a nightmare, of course, in which one of the nuns comes to look round the dormitory when your bed isn't made, and it ought to be. That is what our souls are like, when our Lord comes to visit them in Holy Communion; and we ought to be like the centurion about it: "Yes, Lord, come if you would like to; I am ready to turn anything out to make room for you. But you will find everything in a dreadful mess; and it will always be in a mess until you say your word of command, and I become what *you* want me to be."

CHAPTER 12

Seed-Time

It was for me to plant the seed, for Apollo to water it, but it was God who gave the increase. And if so, the man who plants, the man who waters, count for nothing; God is everything, since it is he who gives the increase. This man plants, that man waters; it is all one. And yet either will receive his own wages, in proportion to his own work. You are a field of God's tilling, a structure of God's design; and we are only his assistants.

With what grace God has bestowed on me, I have laid a foundation as a careful architect should; it is left for someone else to build upon it. Only, whoever builds on it must be careful how he builds.
(1 Cor. 3:6–10)

SAINT PAUL WAS, AS WE ALL KNOW, A BRAVE MAN IN MANY ways. And in one respect he had a courage which few people share nowadays: he was never afraid of mixing his metaphors. In those words I have just read to you he is juggling with two metaphors, one in each hand, so to speak, that of the farmer who sows his grain, and that of the architect who lays his foundations. Suppose that a great architect had laid the foundations, just the foundations, of a new Catholic cathedral, and then he had got a letter to say that after all the Archbishop had decided to dispense with his services, and was giving the contract to a cheap and nasty architect instead. Think what that would be like. It is not a thing that happens to architects very often; but it's the same thing, exactly the same thing, that happens to the Christian teacher. He lays a foundation in the hearts of those who hear him, and then there is nothing more for him to do. He must simply sit by and twiddle his thumbs and watch them make a mess of it.

Or take the position of the farmer. The farmer really does have that experience, and has it every year. He ploughs the land and harrows it and manures it and throws the seed into the ground, and then has to hang about waiting for it to come up, not knowing in the least how it is going to do, or what return he will get for his outlay. He doesn't know what the weather is going to be like between March and the summer, and that may make all the difference. And then there's the wireworm which may come along and spoil his crop; and school-children who will leave the gates open so that the cattle get in from the next field and trample it all down, and other natural pests of the same sort. And that is exactly the position of the Christian teacher; he sows his seed in the hearts of those who listen to him, and then he has nothing to do but hang about watching the signs of the weather and trembling at the frosts until something comes up. There's no tragedy in the world like this constant tragedy of the teaching profession. Everybody else who is an artist in any way has merely to impress his own ideas upon dead materials, canvas or clay; and if anything goes wrong there is nobody but himself to blame for it. But the teacher works upon living materials,

The Gospel in Slow Motion

and depends, for results, on their cooperation. That was St. Paul's tragedy. All his epistles are written to people he had taught, people who had only taken a couple of years or so to forget all that he had taught them. It is that incorrigible forgetfulness of theirs which, you will find, in the epistle to the Galatians, for example, makes St. Paul, saint though he was, come very near to losing his temper. He is like a schoolmaster or a schoolmistress at the end of term, and we all know how near schoolmasters and schoolmistresses do come to losing their temper, at the end of term.

Perhaps we had better keep to one metaphor at a time; let us stick to the farming metaphor. Our Lord himself uses it many times, most notably in the parable of the sower, which comes on Sexagesima Sunday. (Notice how topical Sexagesima Sunday always is; it has a gospel about sowing, just when the farmers are beginning to think when they will start sowing, and the lessons in the first nocturn at Matins are all about the Flood, just when the farmers are beginning to wonder whether it will ever stop raining.) It isn't surprising, after all, that the work of the Christian teacher should be, like that of the farmer, a work involving anxious expectation and frequent disappointment. Because, in a sense, Almighty God himself is handicapped in the same way, in his dealings with us, his refractory children. He, too, lavishes his grace upon men, and watches them squander and misuse it, and does not interfere. There is a sense, of course, in which all human action is the direct outcome of the Divine will; there is a sense in which you can say that grace does everything. That is why in the parable of the cockle and the wheat you hear about a field which apparently consists of uniform soil from end to end; two different crops are sown in it; the wicked, who are the children of the devil, and the just, who are the children of God. That parable throws into relief the action of Divine grace; the parable of the Sower gives you the other side of the picture, throws into relief the action of human free will. Here it is the same seed, apparently, which is sown all over the field; but it doesn't come up the same everywhere, because, as it falls in this part of the field or that, it finds different kinds of soil to lodge in. Almighty God has granted us human beings free will, and he is determined not to destroy the freedom of our wills by interfering, all the time, to prevent us making fools of ourselves. And therefore Almighty God himself may, in a sense, be compared to a disappointed farmer, looking for results which don't come. There is only one thing in creation which is ever wasted, absolutely wasted, can never be useful even as scrap: and that is, God's grace when he bestows it on a soul which doesn't correspond with it, doesn't make any use of it; grace refused is something simply thrown away.

You, says St. Paul to the Corinthians, are a field of God's tilling; we—he means himself and his fellow-teachers—are God's assistants. Since God has decided to let man work out his own salvation, to let him accept grace or reject it as he will, no wonder that those who work as helpers on God's farm, his priests and all those who look after human souls, should meet with constant disappointments, like the disappointments of the farmer. And in the gospel of the sower you find a rapid sketch drawn by our Lord himself of what those disappointments are, and what is the cause of them. I preached you a sermon very much like this last year. It is not exactly the same sermon, but it is on the same lines—it has to be. You see, our Lord himself has given us sermon notes of this parable of the

The Gospel in Slow Motion

Sower; has told us what every detail in the story means. So you wouldn't be likely to get a brand-new sermon on the parable of the Sower, from me or from anybody else.

A sower went forth to sow. I hope you won't think I am adopting an offensively elderly manner if I tell you that you are at the seed-time of your lives; school-time is seed-time. Your characters are the soil to which the good seed is being committed. And the nuns here are God's helpers in his work of tillage. I'm not thinking simply of the classes in which you learn about religion; I'm thinking of the whole complex of religious influences which surrounds you here from morning till night. The question is: How much is it going to sink in? In the parable, some of the grain fell by the wayside; that is, I suppose, on the headland, the strip of unploughed earth at the edge of the field, or perhaps some path across the field, beaten hard by the steps of many passers-by. The sower in the parable obviously does things in a rather slap-dash way; he doesn't always look where he's sowing; and the result of that is that some of the grain is wasted on the hard path. Naturally the birds get it before there is any chance of its finding a crack to bury itself in. Probably there's a scarecrow in the field, but it won't keep all the birds away all the time. Well, at most schools there are some people who are just like that path; they seem to have nothing but brick-bats under their skins. I hope there's nobody like that here; but if there is, all the religion of the place is going to be wasted on her. The devil takes it away, our Lord says—the birds, you see, represent the devil. And it's easy to see who the scarecrow is; I'm the scarecrow, saying Mass for you every morning; but that's not going to prevent the devil undoing all the good you might get at this place, if you shut yourself up like an oyster and refuse to be influenced. I've known people at Catholic schools who were, or seemed to be, like that; and I've met people at Oxford who, when they were at school, had been or said they'd been like that; and I know what becomes of them. They resisted the influence of their school, and the religion which was taught at it. Mass attendance was a mere routine to them, Confession a formality, their whole attitude towards religion a kind of dazed acquiescence. They could talk smoothly and say the proper things, they'd picked up all the outward tricks of the place, but they'd never tried to reach its heart, to read its secret. Are you like that? Spring is coming, Lent is coming; you need the plough.

And other seeds fell on rocky land, where the soil was shallow; they sprang up all at once, because they had not sunk deep into the ground; but as soon as the sun rose they were parched; they had taken no root, and so they withered away. That's far commoner; terribly common, I'm afraid, in our Catholic schools. You don't resist the influence of religion—why should you? It's all quite natural, quite unembarrassing. Go to Communion several times a week; of course; why not? Say a prayer in front of our Lady's statue now and again; there's nothing wrong with that, is there? It's all as easy as ABC. The heresies of Arius and Nestorius and other people with confusingly similar names, heard dimly in your Christian doctrine class, don't appeal to you as either probable or interesting; you have been told about the heathen worshipping mumbo-jumbo, but you have never felt inclined to imitate them. Of course not; you're a Catholic, and a jolly fine religion too. Yes, but, look here, it's got to go deeper than that. Your religion has got to be a personal religion, something that you carry about with you, that you are prepared to make sacrifices for, that means something to you. Otherwise it won't last. While you are here, remember, the seed is under the ground still, mercifully sheltered from sun and wind and frost; that won't go on for ever. When you leave school, you will emerge rather self-consciously into a large world outside it, feeling rather like a blade of corn just poking its head out to see whether the frosts have stopped yet. The sun is beginning to spring up, the sun of the world's influence—the world which thinks that one religion is as good as another, and that is not saying much; that we only live once, and we are here to enjoy ourselves, and so on. You will make friends with people of all sorts; perhaps you will fall in love, and want to marry somebody whose whole outlook on life is quite different from yours. And now, did that seed ever really strike root? Or was there just a thin layer of earth over the hard rock of an unconverted heart? You are letting yourself in for trouble of conscience, and perhaps for disaster, later on, if you don't see to it that your religion strikes deep, while you are here; if you are content to form a casual school acquaintance with our Blessed Lord, while you are here, instead of a friendship that will last a lifetime.

And even if there is depth of earth, even if the blade is well rooted, that isn't all the crop. Others fell among thorns, and the thorns grew up and choked it. Our Lord has told us what the thorns are; they are the cares and pleasures and riches of this life. They are there already, you see; but it's only later that they will grow up and threaten to dominate your life. People often talk and write as if one's schooldays were a carefree time of life; but of course they're wrong. Gray, for instance, in his ode on a distant prospect of Eton College, said, "Alas, unconscious of their doom, the little victims play"; but,

RONALD KNOX

you know, if you get a close-up view of the young gentlemen at Eton College, they all look as if the world were coming to an end and they were hanged if they saw how they were going to do anything about it. One does worry at school; over small things, petty ambitions, jealousies, grudges, grievances. And one does have pleasures at school; short-lived, perhaps, and insignificant, but exciting enough to keep one awake at night. And one even has the management of one's money in a small way, to use it generously or stingily, wisely or wastefully. And these little cares, and pleasures, and riches can easily breed in you a habit of selfishness, which will be hardly noticeable here—people will laugh it off as something that doesn't matter much, at your age. But such a habit of selfishness may grow into a very large influence, and a very ugly influence in your life. It will be magnified to scale, when you grow up. And if you have turned into a really selfish person, it's quite possible that you will come across circumstances in which self-interest will be pitted against the interests of your religion; and self-interest will win. Watch those thorns.

Well, that's all right, isn't it? You've listened to those three descriptions of unfruitful lives, and you feel quite certain that none of them is meant for you? Quite certain? Thank God. And now you can really get to work. Now you can consider whether the good seed is going to spring up thirty-fold, or sixty-fold, or a hundred-fold in you. You have a life to be lived, a world to be edified, a work to be done; thirty, or sixty, or a hundred; which is it to be? ...You don't get much rest from your religion, do you, as a Catholic? Perhaps not. But the religion which claims you, Christ sowed in tears, and martyrs have watered it with their blood.

CHAPTER 13

A Caution

You know well enough that when men run in a race, the race is for all, but the prize for one; run, then, for victory. Every athlete must keep all his appetites under control; and he does it to win a crown that fades, whereas ours is imperishable. So I do not run my course like a man in doubt of his goal; I do not fight my battle like a man who wastes his blows on the air. I buffet my own body, and make it my slave; or I, who have preached to others, may myself be rejected as worthless.

Let me remind you, brethren, of this. Our fathers were hidden, all of them, under the cloud, and found a path, all of them, through the sea; all alike, in the cloud and in the sea, were baptized into Moses' fellowship. They all ate the same prophetic food, and all drank the same prophetic drink, watered by the same prophetic rock which bore them company, the rock that was Christ. And for all that, God was ill pleased with most of them. (1 Cor. 9:24–27, 10:1–5)

TO MOST OF US, THE SUNDAY EPISTLES ARE PRETTY HIDeously unintelligible. Partly because they are chopped up in such an extraordinary way, always starting in the middle of a paragraph and usually ending in the middle of another paragraph. Partly because

RONALD KNOX

St. Paul was a very difficult sort of correspondent; his mind moved quicker than his pen, and he was always assuming that it would be clear what he was referring to when it often wasn't. Partly because we haven't got the letter which the Corinthians, for example, had written to St. Paul, so there is often a lost clue. Like when you get a letter from casual acquaintances which says "Goo-goo sends her love," and can't remember whether Goo-goo is the nickname of one of the daughters, or whether it's the pet goat. Partly because the people who translated St. Paul's Greek into Latin weren't always terribly good at understanding Greek. Partly because the people who translated the Latin into English thought the more literal they were the better; which is all very well if you are trying to learn Latin by following the liturgy with an English translation; but if you are trying to understand what it is all about, the effect is not so good. If you get a sentence in Latin like *Cicero dixit actum esse de republica*, the proper way of translating that is, "Cicero said it was all over with the Republic." But if you come across a quite literal translation of the Latin, it runs, "Cicero said it to have been all done concerning the public thing," which isn't so helpful. And our English translation of the Bible is sometimes a bit like that. So occasionally I give you my own translation, based on the Greek as well as the Latin, to give you some idea of what St. Paul was talking about.

Well, in the case of the epistle just quoted, what *had* the Corinthians been writing about to make St. Paul first of all represent himself as an athlete who ran "not at an uncertainty," and then to wander off into a long story about the Israelites in the wilderness being followed about by a rock? The Corinthians had been putting various questions to St. Paul, one of which was this: "We are

The Gospel in Slow Motion

rather tied up to know what to do about meat which has been sacrificed to idols. Some of us are very scrupulous, and if they go out to lunch and their host says, 'That saddle of mutton you're eating was a bargain; I picked it up almost as good as new at the temple of the goddess Aphrodite,' they get all hot and bothered about it, and say they're very sorry but their doctor won't allow them to *touch* mutton. Others go to the opposite extreme, and are very lax about it all. They don't even mind sitting down and having a good blow-out in Aphrodite's temple; because they say after all they only go there for the sake of the food, and what is Aphrodite? Just a silly fairy-tale, so it can't matter whether the mutton has been offered in sacrifice to her or not; the important thing is it's been offered to them, and they're going to eat it." That was the situation at Corinth; and St. Paul naturally tells them what you or I would have told them, that one certainly oughtn't to be scrupulous, but on the other hand one's got to draw the line somewhere. It would be silly never to eat a piece of meat without getting a certificate from the butcher that it had never seen the inside of a heathen temple. On the other hand, if Christians play a hearty knife and fork when a public luncheon is being given in honour of a pagan goddess, there are two dangers to be considered. One is that the pagans will think Christians don't take their religion very seriously. And the other is that Christians, mixing so freely with their neighbours and getting into their neighbours' bad habits, will gradually drift away and lose the faith altogether.

Here, St. Paul is concerned to discuss that second danger, the danger of apostasy. And he is particularly concerned to warn the Corinthians against being too cock-a-hoop about their religion, thinking they are such jolly fine Christians that nothing is ever going to upset *their* faith. And he begins by talking about himself. He compares himself to a runner who is in for an important race, or to a boxer who is training for a match. I don't suppose St. Paul was a great patron either of the turf or of the ring, but, you see, he was writing to Corinth, and Corinth was one of the four places in Greece where the big athletic events came off. So he thought he would use metaphors which these Corinthian people would understand.

One's first impression on reading all that is that St. Paul is telling the Corinthians not to be greedy. Lent is just ahead of us, and we picture him as telling the Corinthians that they ought to give up sweets. But of course that isn't the point at all. I have no doubt that St. Paul did eat very sparingly, and when he tells us that he buffeted his own body, I should think it's quite likely that means that he took the discipline. But the reason why he mentions all that is simply this—he wants to make the Corinthians realize that he, an apostle, who has given up so much in order to be a Christian, doesn't take his own salvation for granted; he lives in the full consciousness that he, Paul, if he's not very careful, may go to the bad, may lose his soul. To be a Christian doesn't mean that you are necessarily going to heaven; it only means that you have put down your name for a race, not that you have won it. It only means that you are billed to fight in an important match, not that you've already won the match, and can afford to blow yourself out on champagne and oysters. It's no good starting in the race if you're going to skip about all over the place picking daisies, instead of keeping your eyes on the finish. It's no good being advertised all over the town as Punching Paul, if you don't take the trouble to keep your wind sound and your eye

The Gospel in Slow Motion

steady. No good competing if you are going to fail at the test; even if all that you miss is a crown of pine-leaves, such as the victor was awarded at Corinth. And what of us, if we miss the immortal garlands of heaven?

That, I say, is St. Paul's point; to be a Christian doesn't just mean to accept Christ; it means to *live* Christ, to hold on to your religion like grim death, not allowing yourself little liberties which may mean that charity grows cold, and faith dim. And he proceeds to illustrate that same point by a quite different illustration, which forms the second part of today's epistle. Look at the Israelites in the desert; you would think, wouldn't you, that these people who have left Egypt behind, all the comforts as well as the discomforts of it, and set out in search of a promised land, were proof against every temptation to look back? Having once shaken the dust of Egypt from their feet, having once taken the plunge into the Red Sea—that is how St. Paul thinks of it; it reminds him, you see, of baptism—they were bound to reach their goal without a hitch. But no, it was possible to make a mess of the thing, and sure enough the Israelites did make a mess of the thing. God did all he possibly could for them, he fed them miraculously with bread from heaven, gave them drink miraculously out of a rock; just as later he gave the Corinthians, just as now he gives you and me, miraculous food and drink in the Blessed Sacrament. Baptized in the Red Sea, supernaturally sustained on their journey, the Israelites made a mess of it; and so would the Corinthians make a mess of it, if they weren't careful; and so will you and I make a mess of it, if *we* aren't careful. They were condemned, because they were so unbelieving, because they were so rebellious, to wander up and down in the wilderness, and die there, without ever reaching the Promised Land. And you and I can—God grant we may not—make such a mess of our lives on earth that when we die we shall spend an eternity wandering up and down without God, and never see heaven at all.

What does St. Paul mean by saying that they drank of "the same prophetic rock which bore them company, the rock that was Christ"? The story of Moses hitting the rock twice with his stick, whereupon a stream of water came out, enough to give drink to the Israelites and to their cattle, comes in the Book of Numbers. But the Book of Numbers says nothing whatever about the rock following them round. Apparently that was a story which had grown up among the Jews afterwards. You get the story in some of the writings of the Jewish Rabbis; the rock, they say, was rather like a bee-hive; it was a complete sphere, and rolled round and round, following them on their journeys; when they pitched their tents, it stopped rolling, and they could come and get water from it. I must say that that rather exaggerates the miracle, although at the same time it gives you a rather engaging picture. Did St. Paul believe in that story, do you think? He may have. Or he may have simply called it "the travelling rock" by force of habit, without stopping to think whether he believed in the story or not. Or it's possible that he didn't believe in the story as a literal fact, but intended his remarks to be taken in a mystical sense, because he goes on, you see, to say "the rock was Christ." Possibly he means them to understand, "That old story about the rock which followed the Israelites wherever they went, has really come true for us Christians. For us, the Rock is Christ; from his wounded side, as he hung on Calvary, flowed and flows the sacramental grace which is still with us every day, which is with us in every part of the world." That may have been what he meant, because, as I say, his mind moved quicker than his pen, and he sometimes expected his readers to be rather brisk and intelligent.

Well, I can't promise you that I shall always produce a moral from St. Paul's epistles which will be exactly the moral you need, so that you will sit up each time and say, "Coo! that's me." I don't know, for example, that *this* epistle is particularly meant for you in your circumstances and at your time of life. I don't simply mean that in your circumstances and at your time of life you don't feel any very strong temptation to eat meat which has been offered to idols; because that applies equally to grown-up persons. Our instinct nowadays is to prefer meat which is doing duty for the first time; and if you wanted meat which had been offered to idols you'd find it hard to get, even if you advertised in the papers for it. No, but it doesn't need very much intelligence to make you see that what St. Paul says here about second-hand meat applies to lots of other situations of the same kind. All that he says applies in general to Christian people in any age who live in the middle of, and mixed up with, a pagan civilization. And I'm afraid that is our position nowadays; it isn't just a Protestant country, it's a very largely pagan country that you are growing up in, and you can't expect to get to heaven by simply doing what your neighbours do. Some of you, who come across non-Catholic relations and friends in the holidays, have probably begun to realize that already. All of you will realize it later on.

St. Paul's main principle about Christians living in a pagan society is a very simple one; it's the last sentence of our passage from the epistle; "she that thinketh herself to stand, let her take heed lest she fall." You know how easy it is, when you get frosty days like these after mild weather like we've been having, to come out of the front door and tread jauntily on the top step, only to find yourself, quite unexpectedly, in a sitting position on the bottom step, feeling as if the top of your spine had got mixed up with your back hair. That danger of sudden collapse, St. Paul says, ought to be in our minds continually when we are thinking about our eternal salvation. We are all weaker than we know, stand on more slippery ground than we know, and it doesn't do to take risks. Suppose when you get older somebody wants to marry you, and you aren't frightfully in love with him but you don't exactly mind him, and, after all, you reflect, you can't afford to be choosy about it—yes, I know, but what sort of man really is he? What does he really think about religion, when he isn't playing up to you simply because he's in love with you? Have you really got enough religion for two, if it should prove that he's got no religion at all? Are you really strong enough in your faith to stand up to continual nagging and bantering about it, if it should turn out that he actually dislikes your religion? Don't, if such a situation arises, be too ready to give yourself the benefit of the doubt. Remember St. Paul, one of the best servants our Lord has ever had, slogging away with his eyes on the finish of the race and saying to himself, "I wonder if I can make it? I wonder if that crown is really meant for me?" Remember the Israelites, just a few days' march from Egypt, grousing about their desert food and kneeling down to worship a golden calf. We are all weaker than we know; don't let us throw away our chances by saying, "There's not much wrong with a Catholic like me!"

CHAPTER 14

The No-Men

*These are two anointed ones who stand before
the Lord of the whole earth.* (ZACH. 4:14)

I'M GOING TO TALK TO YOU ABOUT TWO GREAT SAINTS: St. John Fisher and St. Thomas More, the two most influential people, in their day, among the ranks of the English martyrs. I don't expect that the subject of the English martyrs provokes any great enthusiasm in you. Partly because you feel you've heard it all before; I hope you have. And partly because it sounds too much like history; and, with the exams on, history is a thing you would prefer to forget about; or rather it is a thing you *do* forget about, and would prefer not to have to remember about. And it makes people feel such a long way away, when you see pictures of them dressed up in hats that look like large penwipers, and are told to imagine them using old-fashioned English, "Marry-come-up" and "By-my-halidom" and all that sort of business. Well, history isn't really so remote as all that. There are people living now who are more than a hundred years old; those people were already alive when Cardinal Newman was received into the Church. When he was received into the Church, there were people alive, over a hundred, who had been alive a hundred years before, when Prince Charles Edward tried to get back his Father's throne in the '45; he started out from France two hundred years ago next Friday. And in that year, 1745, there were people still alive who could remember King Charles I being defeated at the battle of Naseby. And in *that* year, the year of Naseby, if there was anybody as old as a hundred and ten—and I expect there were, because there were no motors then to knock people down, and there was no wireless to drive them mad—if there was anybody as old as a hundred and ten, he had been alive when St. John Fisher and St. Thomas More went to the scaffold. That's history.

Well, I'm not going to tell you a lot about those two saints. I expect you know a good deal about them already; one of you is descended from one of them. I just want you to seize on one splendid quality about them; their utter independence of mind. You see, the really curious thing about the English martyrs is that there were so few of them. Here you have a completely Catholic country which in a matter of twenty years or so goes Protestant, and nobody seems to mind very much. Why weren't all the other people martyrs too? And the answer to that question is the same as the answer to the question Why did the Germans ever let the Nazis get into power?—you can give it in four words: most men are sheep. You can get them to accept anything, by bluffing them, by bullying them, by applying soft soap when it's needed. But there are a few of the important people in any generation to whom you can't do that. They are not stupid enough to be hoodwinked by propaganda. They are too honest to be bribed with preferment. And they have just that touch of hardness about their minds which won't consent to sacrifice principle for the sake of general peace and calm. You can do nothing with such people, except martyr them. Such were St. John Fisher, and St. Thomas More. Don't run away with a wrong impression of them; they weren't disagreeable sort of people in the literal sense; that is, in the sense, that they were fond of disagreeing with their fellow-men. They weren't cranks with a passion for writing letters to *The Times* every day, not a bit of it. You couldn't have had a more human, companionable friend than St. Thomas More, a jollier host, a more open-minded critic of the world around him. Nor must you suppose that these men, either of them, were backwoods Conservatives, Colonel Blimps, with the fixed idea that what had been good enough for their grandfathers must be good enough for them. On the contrary, they were in the very van of the progressive movement. In the great revival of learning that was taking place just then, St. John Fisher took an enormous part, and kept on building colleges and getting other people to build colleges at the university. It's true that he always built them at Cambridge, which strikes some of us as bad taste; but probably Cambridge needed them more. Anyhow, this is quite certain—that if these two men took a different line from most of their contemporaries, it wasn't because they were tiresome, cross-grained people, and it wasn't because they were people who disliked everything that was modern, and went about saying, "What I mean to say is, what?" They were men loved by their fellows, and typical of their age. That is why they were martyred. If they had been less representative people, they would have been left alone.

I have been insisting on that, partly because it enormously enhances the credit of their performance. Mr. Belloc has written very well on that point. He writes of St. Thomas—and it was equally true of St. John—as follows: "To allow oneself to be killed, of one's own choice, in full life, rather than pay the price of yielding upon one dry, narrow, intellectual point; having, to sustain one…neither enthusiasm within, nor the sense of agreement from others without, this is to die alone indeed! He had no enthusiasm for the Papacy; all his life he had been a reformer in the full sense of the word…. Nor was this extraordinary man supported from without…. The average Englishman had little concern with the quarrel between the crown and Rome; it did not touch his life. The Mass went on just the same, and all the splendours of religion…. To the ordinary man of that day anyone, especially a highly-placed official, who stood out against the King's policy, was a crank…. No, he was not supported from without."

If you want to realize how lonely these two men must have felt in making their protest against the tyranny of King Henry, you have only to look at the sort of way More's wife talked about it, when she went to visit him in prison. "I marvel," she said, "that you, that hitherto have been taken for a wise man, will now so play the fool, to lie here in this close, filthy prison, and be content to be thus shut up among rats and mice, when you might be abroad at your liberty, and with the favour and goodwill both of the king and his council, if you would but do as all the bishops and best learned men of his realm have done. And seeing that you have at Chelsea a right fair house, your library, your gallery and all other necessaries so handsome about you, where you might in the company of me, your wife, your children and household be marry, I muse what in God's name you mean, here still thus fondly to tarry." This was More's second wife, and she wasn't the ancestress of anybody here, so there is no reason why we should be specially polite about her. But I think it is fair to remember that her point of view was probably the common point of view about the line More was taking. And it was worse when his daughter Margaret came and tried to talk him round, because she was a really good woman and he was very fond of her.... Put this question to yourself for a moment. If your father, or someone you were very fond of, was in prison, and about to be martyred on a point of conscience, would you advise him to stick to his point of conscience? Or would you advise him to cave in? ... Life *is* difficult, isn't it?

I say then that John Fisher and Thomas More deserve credit, not only for their martyrdom but for the loneliness of their martyrdom. They were taking their stand on a mere point of principle. They were asked to take an oath promising allegiance to the heirs of Anne Boleyn. They didn't object to doing that; but the oath had a preamble attached to it, which asserted that the king was head of the Church in England; and they held that if they took the oath, they would be understood as giving their assent, not only to the oath itself, but to this heretical preamble as well. They were men of conscience, men of principle. The ordinary Englishman disliked Anne Boleyn very much, and was quite prepared to throw stones at her in the street; but all this business about whether the king was head of the Church, and if so in what sense, seemed to him just boring; let it go, things would come out all right in a few years' time. That is where they were wrong, and the martyrs were right. In a little over twenty years' time the Catholic religion had been suppressed, and the same people who had thrown stones at Anne

RONALD KNOX

Boleyn were throwing up their caps and shouting hooray for Anne Boleyn's daughter, Queen Elizabeth, who took very much after her mother. You can jockey people into anything.

"Well," you say, "that's all ancient history. It's got nothing to do with *us*; the sort of problems which bothered people early in the sixteenth century don't bother *us*." Well, in a sense that's true. Nobody bothers nowadays about the King, God bless him, being Head of the Church in England. It tickles the English citizen to read in the paper that their Majesties attended divine worship yesterday at Sandringham. "Sooner it was them than me," he reflects; but on the whole he rather likes the Church of England to be part of the set-up of monarchy in this country; it gives him a solid sense of prosperity. But as to King George being supreme Head of the Church, he bothers about it as little as King George himself. In that sense, the whole controversy which cost More and Fisher their lives is a dead controversy now. But in a more general sense, we haven't nearly finished with it. It was all part of that general attack of Satan against the Catholic Church, which started immediately after our Lord's death, and is going on still.

Satan, like so many half-educated people, likes to be thought original, but he's really repeating himself all the time in slightly different ways. You will find that about your own temptations, if you look into them; you imagine at first sight that he's really pulled off something absolutely new on you, and then, when you trace it back a bit, you find it was just the same old story, the same kind of pride, the same kind of carelessness, which had landed you several times before. And so it has been with his grand attack on the Christian Church. For the first few centuries it was the Roman emperors that

The Gospel in Slow Motion

were the trouble; Christians were persecuted because they wanted to worship God instead of worshipping the Roman emperor. The Roman Empire fell, and there was a pause, a good long pause, and kings began to become important all over Europe; so Christians like St. John and St. Thomas were persecuted because they wanted to obey God instead of obeying the king. Nowadays, kings are at a discount, and the modern world has started to worship a dreadful thing called the State. Fascism or Communism, it's all the same thing really; it's just worship of the State. And because they hold out against this worship of the State, because they won't let the State dictate to them how they are going to worship and how the Church is going to be organized, people are being killed now all over Europe. We heard plenty about it when it was the Nazis who were doing it; we don't hear so much about it now that it isn't the Nazis. But the thing is going on; more and more the shadow of atheism is falling over the whole of eastern Europe. And it is quite on the cards that within your lifetime the main strength of the Catholic Church will lie in the English-speaking countries; the very countries we have been accustomed to think of as Protestant! France, Spain, Italy, Belgium—you can't bet what is going to happen there. It's quite probable that *you*, later on, will find yourself having to pull your socks up, and help to save the Catholic Church, humanly speaking, from going under.

That's why I want to appeal to you all, as you remember the English martyrs, to cultivate jealously and watchfully your own independence of mind. Don't, whatever you do, grow up into a yes-woman. I don't mean that you should never say Yes; that would make it difficult for you to get married. But learn to distrust yourself the moment you find yourself saying things, and, as the result of saying them often enough, actually thinking things, merely because other people around you are saying them, and perhaps thinking them. You live in a frightful age of propaganda; books, newspapers, and above all the wireless are trying hard all the time to influence your mind; and a great deal of that propaganda is directed in a steady stream against the Catholic religion. Not openly, but in an insidious way; the worshippers of the State are always so selecting and so presenting the news that the Catholic Church always gets mixed up with what is unpopular at the moment, always appears as the enemy of liberty and of progress. It's a highly elaborate business, and oh, it's boring! But *you* are going to live in a world which swallows all that sort of dope; you will find your friends in that world, and possibly, in spite of all the nuns can do to prevent it, your husband. If you're going to be a yes-woman, I don't say that you'll lose the faith, but you'll be a passenger; you'll be no use to the Church, when she wants you. Keep your independence of mind; only half believe what you hear; suspend judgement, think for yourself, learn for yourself. If I am privileged to meet any of you later on, I don't very much mind what else has happened to you; you may be stout, and plain, and your fingernails may be the colour of tomato ketchup, if *only* you've preserved your independence of mind. God bless you all, and give you grace to do it.

CHAPTER 15

Resolutions

The spiritual gifts we have differ, according to the special grace which has been assigned to each. If a man is a prophet, let him prophesy as far as the measure of his faith will let him. The administrator must be content with his administration, the teacher, with his work of teaching, the preacher, with his preaching. Each must perform his own task well; giving alms with generosity, exercising authority with anxious care, or doing works of mercy smilingly.

Your love must be a sincere love; you must hold what is evil in abomination, fix all your desire upon what is good. Be affectionate towards each other, as the love of brothers demands, eager to give one another precedence. I would see you unwearied in activity, aglow with the Spirit, waiting like slaves upon the Lord; buoyed up by hope, patient in affliction, persevering in prayer; providing generously for the needs of the saints, giving the stranger a loving welcome. Bestow a blessing on those who persecute you; a blessing, not a curse. Rejoice with those who rejoice, mourn with the mourner. Live in harmony of mind, falling in with the opinions of common folk, instead of following conceited thoughts; never give yourselves airs of wisdom. (ROM. 12:6–16)

RONALD KNOX

IN THE DOUAY VERSION, WHICH YOU HAVE HEARD ALL your lives, this passage has eight sentences in it, and of those only two have any main verb in them. And even you must know about putting main verbs in sentences. THE CAT SAT ON THE MAT is a sentence, but THE CAT ON THE MAT isn't a sentence, and THE CAT SITTING ON THE MAT isn't either. Well, let me read you the first sentence in the old translation; and when we get to the main verb, will you all cough? "Brethren, having different gifts, according to the grace that is given us, either prophecy, to be used according to the rule of faith, or ministry, in ministering; or he that teacheth, in doctrine, he that exhorteth, in exhorting, he that giveth, with simplicity, he that ruleth, with carefulness, he that sheweth mercy with cheerfulness"—that is the end of the sentence, and there has been no main verb yet. And, main verb or no main verb, what on earth does it all mean?

Well, as usual the trouble to start with is that about half the epistle is off the map, and we start more or less in the middle of a sentence. St. Paul has been saying, what St. Paul was fond of saying, "For heaven's sake do try to quarrel less." It may seem to you very odd that the Christians in Rome, of all places, should want to be given that sort of advice; but then, Christians in Rome aren't always particularly edifying. Like the Irish priest when they pointed out to him that something or other he did was forbidden by the rubrics, and he drew himself up and said, "Rubrics? Rubrics? Haven't I been to Rome, and seen the chaps that made them?" Anyhow, the Christians at Rome had been quarrelling in St. Paul's time, and he says the trouble is really that Christians will not mind their own business. Christians ought to be like the human body, in which the

The Gospel in Slow Motion

hand has got its own job to do and does it, and the eye has got its own job to do and does it, and the foot has got its own job to do and does it, and everything goes on swimmingly. You don't find the foot trying to take money out of its trousers pocket, or the hand shoving itself in front of the eye and saying, "Allow me to show you the way!" So it ought to be with us who are members of the Christian body; each of us ought to stick to his own job, and get on with it.

And that is where our passage starts. "Some of you," he says, "are prophets; if so, for goodness' sake let them prophesy. Don't let them try to run the show; that is for the administrator; and in the same way, let the administrator stick to administrating—don't let him start preaching, that is the preacher's job; or teaching school, that is the teacher's job. Don't keep on looking round you to see if the other man is doing his job well; what you have got to bother about is your job, and making sure that that is well done. Some of you are rich people, your job is to put down money generously [that is what 'with simplicity' means]. Some of you are in positions of authority; you must exercise that authority with anxious care. Some of you do works of mercy, go round and visit the sick, or comfort the mourner; you must do it," St. Paul says, "smilingly." The details of all that don't matter much; his point is that each of us ought to keep his or her eyes upon his or her own job; not be always looking round the corner to see whether Sister So-and-so isn't slacking up a bit.

I don't know whether you made any new-year resolutions, but if you did you have probably already forgotten what they were. So let's register these messages St. Paul sent to the Romans as new-year resolutions for ourselves, it isn't quite too late yet. The first is: do your own job, and leave other people to do theirs.

RONALD KNOX

Then the next point is, "Your love must be sincere love; you must hold what is evil in abomination, fix all your desire upon what is good," I think all that goes together; and it tells us to do something which isn't as simple as it sounds—to like the right people, not the wrong people, and for the right reasons, not for the wrong reasons. That piece of advice doesn't apply so much, I think, to our deepest attachments as to our casual contacts. We are all rather apt to persuade ourselves that we like the people who happen to be popular in the world we live in; and we don't ask ourselves whether we really like them, or whether we allow ourselves to flatter and admire them because it is the thing to do, because we find other people doing it. And we are apt to admire people for the wrong reasons, because they happen to amuse us, for example. But it doesn't follow that because So-and-so can imitate the noise made by a train going through a tunnel, she is really a likeable person; is she humble? is she unselfish? That's a second resolution, a difficult one: to try and see people as they really are, and to like what is really likeable in them.

"Be affectionate towards each other, as the love of brothers demands, eager to give one another precedence." That applies to the love of sisters quite as much as to the love of brothers. The Greek is a bit difficult to translate, because the word doesn't properly mean "affectionate"; it means "eager to bestow affection." We are to be fond of being fond of people, we are to like liking people, we are to be lovers of love. We are not to encourage in ourselves a cynical habit of mind which makes us see everybody's weak points and come to the conclusion that it is a mistake to give anybody our confidence and our affection—they'll only let us down. Be frightened if

The Gospel in Slow Motion

you find yourself thinking like that—it means you are getting selfish. No, we must be fond of liking people, and, what comes to the same thing, eager to give one another precedence. Giving people precedence doesn't mean just waiting for them to go through the door first; that is good manners, but it isn't what St. Paul is thinking about. He is thinking about unselfishness. You know that dreadful habit of talking about oneself as "Number One"? Well, that is just what, as Christians, we are not to do. Other people have got to come first in our thoughts; our affection must be going outwards, towards them, not inwards, towards ourselves, or it will lead to all sorts of trouble. So there is a third resolution: I won't think it smart, I won't think it clever, to be a loveless character.

When St. Paul wrote his letters, I imagine he was always frightfully busy. He didn't sit down and write them himself, like you do a day or so after Christmas, when your mother makes you sit down and write round saying thank you for all your Christmas presents. He dictated to somebody else; and I imagine him striding up and down the room, dictating in a great hurry because he had so many other things to think about. And the result of that is, that he doesn't always stick to the point. What he is really thinking about here, as I say, is the duty of Christians towards one another; and in particular how he is to stop the Christians at Rome having rows with one another. But once he starts thinking about what Christians are like, and what Christians ought to be like, he is rather apt to lose his thread. Ideas crowd in upon him, and he says to his secretary, "Tell them this...tell them that," and goes on striding up and down the room. "I would see you unwearied in activity, aglow with the Spirit, waiting like slaves upon the Lord, buoyed up by hope, patient in affliction, persevering in prayer he is filling in his picture of the ideal Christian with a few bold sweeps of the brush, his duty towards God as much as his duty towards his fellow-men. "Aglow with the spirit," literally "bubbling over with the spirit," like kettles just on the boil—that is the idea; he wants them all to be at concert pitch all the time. But let's leave out that part, and stick to what was really St. Paul's point, the attitude of Christian people towards one another.

"Providing generously for the needs of the saints"; really, it means "sharing in the needs of the saints," only that would need a footnote to explain it. St. Paul, as I'm always telling you, thought of the Christian Church as being among other things a big Benefit Society; if poor Christians were hard up, rich Christians would regard these people's debts as their own, and pay them. That is not a common point of view nowadays, except among Christians who are hard up. But I won't badger you about that; because you haven't got a great deal of money of your own so far, and you'll hear quite enough from the clergy about the duty of almsgiving when you have. For the same reason we may as well leave out the next item on St. Paul's list, which is "giving the stranger a loving welcome." Once again St. Paul doesn't tell the Romans to be hospitable; simply, he tells them to be fond of being hospitable. But I don't suppose your mothers would be very grateful to me if you went about asking strangers to come and stay with you in the holidays; so we will leave that part out till you are older.

Then St. Paul goes on, "Bestow a blessing on those who curse you, a blessing, not a curse." Perhaps that isn't a piece of advice which you and I can be expected to take quite literally nowadays,

The Gospel in Slow Motion

if only because people don't actually curse one another very much nowadays, and for that matter they don't bless one another very much nowadays. *I* am expected to bless *you*, of course, when you go away for the holidays; though I'm not asked to curse you when you come back at the beginning of the term, which would make things more symmetrical. But all the same it remains true that when people say nasty things to us or about us our instinctive reaction is to do the same to them. And it remains true that if you manage to sit on your bad temper and laugh it off somehow, you will be glad of it afterwards. Years ago, Mr. Arnold Lunn wrote a book called *Roman Converts*—he was a Protestant in those days—and sent it to me, because I'd known him at Oxford and I suppose he felt I would like to know what he was saying about me. Well, I'd seen the reviews of the book, and I knew that what he had been saying about me wasn't at all complimentary, especially about a book I had written. So I thought out a thoroughly unpleasant answer, and had it all written out in my head, ready for the next day's post; and then next day, for no reason I could make out, I didn't write it after all; I just wrote him rather a nice letter thanking him for sending me *Roman Converts*, and agreeing that the book of mine he had criticized probably was rather a bad book, and I wasn't sure that I should want to publish it now if it hadn't been published already, and so on. Several years afterwards, when Mr. Lunn became a Roman convert himself, he told me that that letter of mine had really made him think quite a lot. I shouldn't mention that story to you if I was in the habit of doing nice things like that; it just happens to stick out in my mind as a solitary instance in which I did take St. Paul's advice; and, as you may imagine, I wasn't sorry for it afterwards.

RONALD KNOX

The next thing is, "Rejoice with those who rejoice, mourn with the mourner." I haven't left myself much time to talk about that; but don't forget (as one of your new-year resolutions) to rejoice with the rejoicer as well as mourning with the mourner. Being sorry for people who are in trouble comes naturally to most of us. But other people's birthdays and prizes and good news from home are rather boring, aren't they? And if we aren't feeling frightfully cheerful ourselves there's a temptation to say, "Oh, really?" Don't be content to say, "Oh, really?" Don't be content with yourself until you find yourself really pleased to hear about other people being happy.

The last sentence is rather obscure; the ordinary translation is, "Being of one mind one towards another; not minding high things, but consenting to the humble"; of course it may mean just that, being content with the society of simple people, like our Lady at Bethlehem telling the shepherds how kind it was of them to come. But I think it means humble things, humble thoughts, rather than humble people. "Live in harmony of mind, falling in with the opinions of common folk, instead of following conceited thoughts that makes it so much easier, you know, for people to live at peace together, if they aren't always trying to be too clever, always trying to be different. Let's make that our last new-year resolution—it comes easier to some of us than to others: not be too clever. And at that point our epistle stops short rather in the middle of things, and tells us to look out for another thrilling instalment next Sunday.

CHAPTER 16

God's Good Marks

But the Lord warned Samuel, Have no eyes for noble mien or tall stature; I have passed this one by. Not where man's glance falls, falls the Lord's choice; men see but outward appearances, he reads the heart. (1 KINGS 16:7)

I DON'T KNOW WHETHER YOU LEARN A LOT ABOUT THE Old Testament here, or only just bits. But I expect even if you only learn bits you have been told about the passage from which *this* text comes, because it is one of the high spots in the Old Testament; it is the passage where Samuel goes off to Bethlehem to find the king he is to anoint instead of King Saul; it is to be one of the sons of Jesse, but he doesn't yet know which. And all Jesse's sons are paraded before him in turn, while he stands there with the horn of oil ready to anoint him, when God says, "This is the one." The first that turns up is Eliab, very impressive and good-looking; and Samuel says to himself, "Obviously this is the man." But no, you see: he is to have no eyes for noble mien or tall stature; not where man's glance falls, falls the Lord's choice. So we have to try again; and another son comes forward, called Abinadab, and then another called Samina, and still it's no use. Seven sons pass by, and still the horn of oil hasn't done its work, and Samuel is beginning to get anxious; it looks as if there had been some mistake. So he turns to Jesse and asks whether all his sons are present and correct; and suddenly it dawns on everybody, "We've forgotten the kid!" There was another son, after all, a boy called David; only his brothers had made him stay at home looking after the sheep while they were getting into their best clothes and clean collars. So Samuel says, "It's no good, we can't go on without *him*"; and David is sent for. And he comes in looking all red in the face and rather pathetic, and the Lord tells Samuel, "Arise, and anoint him, for this is he."

That kind of story is always cropping up in the Old Testament. Joseph was nearly the youngest son of Jacob, and David was quite the youngest son of Jesse; and when Joseph becomes governor of Egypt, and David becomes king of Israel, you sit up and take notice, if you're the youngest of six as I was, and rather apt to be ragged by your elder brothers and sisters. It was the sort of thing that happened in the fairy-stories, of course, just to make them more interesting; the first two brothers in the story were simply so much dragon-fodder, simply because they would not take the obvious precautions; it was always the third brother who killed the dragon and got the princess. But here was a piece of real life—and a very important piece of real life—where the same principle seemed to apply. It was only when you got older, and tried to read the epistle to the Romans with some attempt to understand it, that you realized why it was God's way to choose David and Joseph, not their elders. He wanted to make it clear that his choice didn't depend on human considerations; that his candidate was not the candidate who seemed, on human calculations, the most likely. He wanted to

The Gospel in Slow Motion

make it clear that he could use any material to produce the results he wanted; that the illiterate and the despised could do as well as anybody else if he chose them. "Men see but outward appearances; he reads the heart"; he could see rich capacities buried away in the most unlikely people; and naturally, for who put them there, if not he?

All that helps to remind us that there is a general election coming on. I'm not going to give you any advice about that, because most of you won't be able to vote at it. There's a sort of idea that you are too young; it's a silly idea, of course, but there it is. What I did think, though, was that the general election would be a useful parable to illustrate the thing I'm trying to talk about. Men see but outward appearances, God reads the heart—how ridiculously inadequate, when all is said and done, is the process by which we select one of our fellow-citizens to do what he likes with our lives and our property for the next five years! When I talk of judging by outward appearances, I don't mean that we always vote for the man with the nicest smile or the bushiest moustache; though I believe the standard of good looks among our legislators has noticeably gone up since women got the vote. All I mean is that we really know precious little about them when we elect them, and not a great deal afterwards. We are given our choice between Colonel Smith and Mr. Jones. Colonel Smith stands for a strong army, a determined foreign policy, lots more education (if you care for the idea of that), a revival of agriculture, old-age pensions for everybody at sixty, more employment, and less work. Mr. Jones stands for less work, more employment, old-age pensions for everybody at sixty, a revival of agriculture, lots more education, a determined foreign policy and a strong army. Colonel Smith's agent gets to work, and discovers that Mr. Jones once said he didn't approve of greyhound-racing. Mr. Jones' agent discovers that in 1933 Colonel Smith, in an after-dinner speech, said perhaps Hitler wasn't such a bad chap as people made out. Colonel Smith puts up posters to say HANDS OFF THE PEOPLE'S FUN! and Mr. Jones puts up posters to say A VOTE FOR SMITH IS A VOTE GIVEN TO FASCISM! In the end, Colonel Smith gets in, and makes a little speech to say that he was elected because the British people are determined to preserve their liberties, and Mr. Jones makes a speech to say that it was a clean fight, and his defeat was only due to the apathy of the electorate. And so they drive off, both of them; and what do we really know about either?

Have we any sort of idea whether Colonel Smith is kind to his wife? Have we any sort of evidence whether Mr. Jones goes to church on Sunday morning, or just sits in an armchair with his collar off reading the *News of the World*? Nobody has told us anything it would be at all interesting to *know* about them. At any rate, you say, we know something about their politics. Yes, but do we really even know much about that? Does even Colonel Smith know much about that? In a few months' time he will be voting the way his party leaders tell him to, not the way we told him to. All we really know, or rather guess, from hearing them make election speeches, is that Colonel Smith is probably a relatively honest man, though a bit of an ass, and that Mr. Jones probably means well, in spite of the appalling tie he wears. And we have chosen between them; it will be time to repent our choice five years hence, if we are lucky.

So man makes his choice, when man chooses. How does God make his choice, when God chooses? He sees, among all the

The Gospel in Slow Motion

thousands of Israel, one shepherd boy; very plucky, very cunning—rather too cunning, perhaps, in some ways—a bit sentimental, a bit susceptible; there will be trouble about these things later on; still, he'll do. He'll do, because God will give him the opportunity to use these qualities on the right occasions, because God will give him grace to perfect these qualities as time goes on. Is God choosing a man, or making a man? You can hardly say; that brings you slap up against the mystery of predestination. What you don't know, and God does know, is that this man whom he himself has made, and made to be the kind of man he is, will in fact correspond with the graces that are given him in such a way as to become a hero in Israel, the saviour of his people, the founder of a great dynasty, the type, even, of the Christ who is to come. God isn't taking any risks; he knows that David will commit foolish acts, sins even. But he sees already the complete pattern of David's life, with all these follies and sins woven into it; and he says, "Good, that one will do; I'll take that one." And out comes Samuel's horn, and the oil is pouring all over the untidy hair of the shepherd-boy.

Well, that's enough about the Old Testament; God works just in the same way under the New. He doesn't choose the people we should expect always; doesn't choose the people that have any particular qualifications, as far as we can see, for the job. But he knows what he's doing. Here is a fisherman, who makes his living by the shore of the Lake of Galilee; part owner of a boat, but not with much money; very little education, talking with a strong Galilean accent; not free from worldly ties—he is a married man, and has a mother-in-law to look after who is a bit of an invalid; not really a very promising disciple. But Jesus Christ puts him on his trial;

tells him to go out and let down his nets for a catch of fish in a day when anybody could see no fish were moving. What is his answer? "Master, we have toiled all night and caught nothing; nevertheless at thy word I will let down the net." Good! He'll do; that is the stuff disciples are made of. Oh, there is a lot to be said against him; he is rather a bossy sort of person, apt to boast and to bluster, rushing headstrong into awkward situations and then appealing to be helped out of them; a man who may let you down at a crisis. But he is the man our Lord wants; wants him to be a fisher of men. That rather too-self-confident fisherman is to be the prince of the apostles.

You'd have thought that a curious choice; but our Lord is ready to make more curious choices still. Here is a Jewish student, a frightful type of intellectual, pig-headed and terribly sure of himself, who has got his knife into this new sect that follows the crucified Jesus of Nazareth. He takes on a job as a kind of S.S. man, rushing round and persecuting the unfortunate Christians and hounding them into concentration camps. He is actually on his way to carry out a brutal mission of this sort at Damascus; when suddenly there is a bright light that seems to come out of the sky, there is a mysterious sound—was it thunder? It seemed more like the accents of a human voice. And there is young Saul, thrown from his horse, getting up and groping his way about in complete blindness. What on earth has happened? You may well ask; nothing has happened *on earth*—it's in heaven that something has happened. Quite suddenly, heaven has arranged that this dreadful young man is to become a Christian, and a saint, and one of the most lovable of the saints. It seemed unbelievable at the time; when a Christian convert at

The Gospel in Slow Motion

Damascus was told to go and baptize Saul of Tarsus, he said, "Lord, you can't possibly mean that; he's an awful man, always persecuting us Christians; that's what he's come here for." But it's all right; "Go thy way," our Lord says, "the man is a chosen instrument of mine." A prig and a pedant, fresh from the university, stuffed with all the worst notions imaginable—he is to be the Teacher of the Gentiles.

It's the same story, then, in the New Testament as in the Old; in a hundred guesses, you wouldn't have picked out Peter and Paul as the right men for the job, but Peter and Paul are to be the second founders of Rome, the pillars of the universal Church. We have been talking of the way God chooses, when some frightfully important choice has to be made, when he must have representatives who will not let him down. But of course he doesn't always get representatives who will live up to the splendid destinies he has prepared for them. If he chose King David, he also chose King Saul, who was no use. If he chose Peter and Paul, he also chose Judas, who was worse than no use. You see, he asks for the free consent of our wills if he is to make anything of us, all of us, from our Blessed Lady downwards. You and I probably aren't very important to his purposes. I say probably, because possibly you are all going to be saints; it would be very jolly if you were; but on the law of averages it doesn't seem likely. Many are called, but few chosen; you and I may quite possibly make a mess of our lives. But it is certain that he has a special vocation for you and me, even if it's a rather ordinary one. And he takes into account the sort of people we are, the sort of qualities we have and haven't got, when he designs that vocation for us.

He sees not as man sees; he can read our hearts. You mustn't think of him as just looking down from the sky to see whether we have got bobbles on the top of our berets or not. He can see inside us; Eliab in his clean collar, and David all covered over with bits of wool from getting the sheep out of ditches—it's all the same to him. Other people, the people around us, really know very little about what's going on inside us, even schoolmistresses, who always seem to be watching. And therefore we ought constantly to be reminding ourselves that what other people think of us doesn't matter a rap; they always get us wrong. That is a consoling reflection sometimes, when we feel lonely and misunderstood, and are inclined to mope about it. But I don't know that that kind of moping does much good to us, or to anybody else. No, what is far more important is to be quite unimpressed when other people make a lot of us, and we get a really whopping good report from the nuns at the end of term. When people say nice things about us, our first thought should always be, "Good gracious, I know myself better than that"; and our second thought should be, "God knows me even better than I know myself." His good marks are the only things that really matter; *his* praise is the only thing a sensible person lives for. When we were cheeky and didn't mean to be, he knows we didn't mean to be; when we said the right thing, but only by accident, he knows it was only by accident. He can see your life putting out shoots underground, in answer to the graces he gives you; or lying there all dried up and brown at the edges because you are thinking all the time about other people, not about him.

CHAPTER 17

An Old Favourite

I may speak with every tongue that men and angels use; yet, if I lack charity, I am no better than echoing bronze, or the clash of cymbals. I may have powers of prophecy, no secret hidden from me, no knowledge too deep for me; I may have utter faith, so that I can move mountains; yet if I lack charity, I count for nothing. I may give away all that I have, to feed the poor; I may give myself up to be burnt at the stake; if I lack charity, it goes for nothing. Charity is patient, is kind; charity feels no envy; charity is never perverse or proud, never insolent; does not claim its rights, cannot be provoked, does not brood over an injury; takes no pleasure in wrongdoing, but rejoices at the victory of truth; sustains, believes, hopes, endures, to the last. The time will come when we shall outgrow prophecy, when speaking with tongues will come to an end, when knowledge will be swept away; we shall never have finished with charity. Our knowledge, our prophecy, are only glimpses of the truth; and these glimpses will be swept away when the time of fulfilment comes. (Just so, when I was a child, I talked like a child, I had the intelligence, the thoughts of a child; since I became a man, I have outgrown childish ways.) At present, we are looking at a confused reflection in a mirror; then, we shall see face to face; now, I have only glimpses of knowledge; then, I shall recognize God as he

RONALD KNOX

has recognized me. Meanwhile, faith, hope and charity persist, all three; but the greatest of them all is charity. (1 Cor. 13:1–13)

AS I HAVE ALREADY MENTIONED SEVERAL TIMES, I AM engaged in translating St. Paul's epistles at the moment, and the more I do that the more conscious I become that I have never really begun to understand St. Paul's epistles before. There are a good many things in them I don't understand even now. And, that being so, I feel fairly confident that you don't understand them either. Even this one, which we all know almost by heart, have we really got it properly taped? Do we realize, for example, what the context of it all is? "Oh," you say, "it doesn't matter very much about the context; I suppose the Corinthians were rather a bad lot, and St. Paul thought he would tell them something about charity." Well, you see, that shows you that you have got it all wrong. The Corinthians weren't a bad lot at all, only one or two of them. Most of them were terribly good, quite appallingly good. They had a passion for going to church. And being like that, they spent a very large part of their time quarrelling. The first eight or nine verses of the first chapter in this epistle are occupied with thanking God that they are all so good and holy, and then St. Paul goes straight on to suggest that it would be rather a good thing if they weren't always quarrelling.

Going to church, for the Corinthians, doesn't seem to have meant quite the same thing as it does for us. They did, of course, go to Mass like Christians, but what we hear about their other devotional practices reminds us rather more of a sort of testimony-meeting such as you get among the Nonconformists. You see,

The Gospel in Slow Motion

they had only just been converted to the Christian religion, and they were full of excitement about it, so they simply had to get up and let off steam. And there are two ways of letting off steam with which St. Paul is concerned here; one he calls speaking with tongues, and the other he calls prophesying. You all know that the apostles spoke with tongues on the day of Pentecost. But the thing didn't stop there, apparently. People used to get up at these early Christian prayer meetings and make noises which, to the ordinary listener, were quite unintelligible. Sometimes it appeared that they were talking in a foreign language; sometimes it didn't seem to be any language at all, and then they would say, "Well, I don't suppose it was a human language; it was the language the angels talk." That's what it means when it says, *I may speak with every tongue that men and angels use*. Prophesying sometimes meant foretelling the future, or reading the secrets of other people's hearts, but I should think in the ordinary way it was more like a set of pious ejaculations, forced out of people by the influence of the Holy Spirit—not always, it appears, under the influence of the Holy Spirit; sometimes something went wrong, and the prophecies had to be suppressed. Well, you will see for yourselves that this must have been a rather untidy form of worship at the best of times. But what made it worse was that the Corinthians were so frightfully keen on these spiritual accomplishments of theirs. Several people would get up and speak with tongues at the same time, and you wouldn't get much out of French class if everybody spoke at the same time. Even with prophesying there was the same difficulty. One prophet would get going and nothing would stop him; and the next one who was waiting his turn would get more and more impatient, till finally he couldn't sit quiet any longer, but started prophesying himself without waiting for the one in front of him to finish. I'm not making up all this; you can see that this happened if you read the fourteenth chapter of this epistle, which comes immediately after our passage. And now perhaps you see why St. Paul wanted to write to the Corinthians about charity. You have to read what he says against that background; you have to keep in your mind the picture of the two prophets, one too full of his own message to sit down, and the other too full of his own message to wait till he did.

And what St. Paul tells them is that there is another gift of the Holy Spirit, besides prophesying and talking with tongues and so on, and it is much more worth having; so much so that unless you have got it, no other gift is worth having at all; its name is charity. If you haven't got charity, getting up and making noises in public, whether what you say is intelligible or not, is waste of time; you might as well be beating kettle-drums. I always hope we may assume from this passage that St. Paul wasn't musical, because obviously he thought the noise made by a brass band had no *meaning* at all.

I think it's perhaps rather hard for us to throw ourselves back into the atmosphere of the very early Church, so I propose to go through St. Paul's list of spiritual gifts illustrating it by what we read of God's saints in later times. St. Francis Xavier, who converted all those people out in the East, is said to have spoken, on many occasions, in the language of the people he was trying to convert, without having learned a word of it. That is all right, says St. Paul; it's a splendid testimony to the sanctity of St. Francis Xavier. But only, remember, because he was preaching to the Indians and the

The Gospel in Slow Motion

Chinese out of love for God, and about the love of God, and because he loved the souls of the people he was talking to. If he'd been trying to sell them gin, all his speaking with tongues wouldn't have made a saint of St. Francis Xavier.

And so with the other gifts. *I may have powers of prophecy*—many of the saints had that. When King Totila, the Goth, paid a visit to St. Benedict, who had never met him before, he made one of his soldiers dress up in the royal robes and pretend to be the king; and as soon as St. Benedict saw him, he said, "Take those things off; you know they don't belong to you." That makes a nice story, because St. Benedict lived on roots in a cave to learn the love of God; if he had been a fashionable medium, it would make a very poor story indeed. *No secret hidden from me*—St. Thomas Aquinas, the Dominican, was very good at explaining mysteries; and he wrote an enormous book called the *Summa*, which you will never read. When he had nearly finished it, he had an ecstasy one day as he was saying Mass, and after breakfast, when they told him to get on with the *Summa*, he said he couldn't get interested in it; "everything I have written seems trash, compared with what I've seen, and what has been revealed to me." That never happened to Immanuel Kant, or John Stuart Mill, or any of the Early Victorian philosophers. But even heavenly visions aren't everything; *no knowledge too deep for me*—when St. Paul talks about knowledge, he always means mystical revelations. Take a saint like St. Philip Neri; he used to have an ecstasy every day when he said Mass; it was a regular arrangement that the server should ring the consecration bell, and then go out and have his breakfast and read the paper and come back in about two hours' time, which was just in time to ring the bell again for the *Domine non sum dignus*. Well, if St. Philip had spent those two hours in getting ideas for some book he was writing about mystical theology, that would have been all wrong; that's not what the Mass is for. But he spent those two hours pouring out his soul in love to God, and because it was love it was all right. *I may have utter faith; so that I can move mountains*—St. Gregory Thaumaturgus, a man of great faith, is said to have moved a mountain; not far, but just far enough to make room for the site of a new church; I don't know whether the story is true or not. But, you see, that isn't the point of St. Gregory. The point about him is that when he was dying, he asked how many pagans there were left in his cathedral city of Neocaesarea. And they told him, "There are still seventeen." "Well, thank God," he said; "when I came here there were only seventeen Christians." Dear old man, how he loved God and men!

But it isn't only these miraculous gifts, the *gratiae gratis datae*, that are no good without charity. Heroic generosity is no good without it either. *I may give away all that I have to feed the poor*—no good to do that, unless it is love that does it. Let's have some female saints. St. Elizabeth of Hungary; she gave so much to the poor that her husband said she wasn't to give any more. And then he found her sneaking out with a bundle, and said, "What have you got in there?" which was awkward, because it was full of bread. And St. Elizabeth said, perhaps losing her head rather, "Oh, just some roses," and he said, "Open that bundle," and she did, and they were roses. I suppose if you really love God you can take that sort of risk. *I may give myself up to be burnt at the stake*—St. Anastasia took an even bigger risk; she committed suicide. They were martyring her, and when she saw the fire ready she was so impatient that she

The Gospel in Slow Motion

jumped into it. But it was all right, the theologians tell us, because it was a special inspiration; the fire within her burned more fiercely than the fire without. It's not the bread that matters, it's not the martyrdom that matters, it's the love of God.

Well, at that point you may feel inclined to object, "How can people give all their goods to feed the poor, how can they allow themselves to be burned, without charity? Surely people don't do that sort of thing for fun." Yes, but you see, I think that's intimately concerned with what St. Paul meant by charity. The Greek word *agape* in St. Paul has, I think, nearly always the sense of fellowship, of unity. To keep the unity of the Church unimpaired—that is our first duty, higher than any other. And a man like Peter Waldo, who gave his goods to feed the poor but started the heresy of the Waldenses; men like Latimer and Ridley, who gave their bodies to be burned, but only after helping to force England into schism—people like that were backward in charity.

This unity, this fellowship, this harmony among brethren—this is what counts first and counts most, says St. Paul to the Corinthians. And then he goes on to give a lot of little instances from everyday life to show how charity works out in practice. *Charity is patient*—you know how hard it is to put up with a real bore, for example, but it's got to be done; fellowship demands it. *Is kind*—so hard, sometimes, to forget your own pleasures and attend to somebody else who needs help or comfort, but fellowship demands it. *Feels no envy*—it you really have the spirit of fellowship, it doesn't matter a bit whether it was you or the other girl who scored the goal. *Is never perverse*—doesn't stick to its own opinion, its own way of doing things, follows the opinion of others, for the sake of fellowship. *Is never proud*—we are so tempted sometimes to show off, but it spoils fellowship. *Is never insolent*—how silly rules seem at times, so obviously not made for us! And yet even rules have to be kept; fellowship suffers if they aren't. *Has no selfish aims*—of course not, how could we be selfish, we who love Christ? *Cannot be provoked, does not brood over an injury*—that's more difficult, especially when people lay themselves out to provoke us, but fellowship demands that we should keep our tempers, even then, so as not to introduce feuds into the world we live in. *Takes no pleasure in wrong-doing, but rejoices in the victory of truth*—there is a partisan spirit in all of us, which tempts us to sit by and applaud when the other party is scored off, even if the score wasn't quite a fair one; but that doesn't make for fellowship, the wider fellowship; charity only rejoices when the truth comes out top. Charity *sustains to the last*—any kind of insult or neglect; *believes*—would sooner look a fool by being taken in than try to assert its own intellectual superiority; *hopes*—doesn't mope and get depressed and make itself a wet blanket all round when things seem to be going wrong; *endures*—even when there's no bath-water or when it's the wrong kind of pudding two days running; it's that spirit of rebellion, even in small things, that destroys fellowship so. The lack of those qualities on a larger scale, St. Paul would tell us, have been responsible for all the schisms that have rent the seamless robe of the Church.

The end part of the epistle, about prophecies and knowledge and all that, is pretty clear in the main outlines of its meaning, but the actual phrases of it have got a bit blurred; partly as I say because St. Paul wrote quicker than he thought. "The time will come when we shall outgrow prophecy, when speaking with tongues will come

The Gospel in Slow Motion

to an end, when knowledge will be swept away; we shall never have finished with charity." The time St. Paul is referring to, of course, is when we get to heaven. This gift of talking in foreign languages, which the Corinthians are so proud of, really won't be of any use then. That is a sentiment which I hope you won't use as an argument for not learning the French irregular verbs; they won't be much use to you in heaven, but you've still got to get there. Why won't languages be any use to us in heaven? Because we shan't talk there at all? I'm afraid, for some of us, that would rather take the gilt off the ginger-bread. Or simply in the sense that there will be no need of learning *different* languages, because we shall all talk the same? That would rouse the interesting speculation: What language will it be? Some people, I think, have conjectured that in heaven we shall all talk Hebrew; but I rather hope not; because I've been trying to learn Hebrew for about five years now, and it seems to me a very untidy language.

No, I imagine the real answer is that we shan't need the use of language at all for communicating our thoughts to one another. We shan't need to attract people's attention, and clear our throats, and then waggle our tongues about; we shall short-circuit all that. Long ago, when I was travelling for a week or two in Germany, I wanted to send off a letter from Munich. So I learned very carefully, out of a phrase-book, the sentence, "Will you to me a postage stamp for twenty pfennigs give?" Armed with that sentence, I set out through the town of Munich in search of a post office. But I suppose I was expecting the wrong things, expecting to see a large red hole in the wall somewhere, such as you look for in England; anyhow, I couldn't find a post office. After a long, hot walk I gave it up in despair, and decided to return to the hotel. And just at the corner of the street which led to my hotel, I found an automatic machine, into which you dropped twenty pfennigs and it to you a postage stamp for twenty pfennigs gave. And that, St. Paul would have said, would be the position of one of these highly privileged Corinthians when he got to heaven; he would know his foreign languages all right, but it wouldn't be any use, because the whole thing could be done automatically.

And it was the same, of course, with the power of prophecy, of looking into the future and reading men's hearts; it was the same with knowledge, that imperfect knowledge of heavenly mysteries which was imparted to the Corinthians sometimes in their prayer. "Our knowledge," says St. Paul, "our prophecy, are only glimpses of the truth, and these glimpses will be swept away when the time of fulfilment comes. Just so, when I was a child, I talked like a child, I had the intelligence, the thoughts of a child; since I became a man, I have outgrown childish ways. At present, we are looking at a confused reflection in a mirror; then, we shall see face to face; now, I have only glimpses of knowledge, then, I shall recognize God as he has recognized me." Of course, you wouldn't remember what it was like being a child—it's too long ago; I mean, when you liked playing with toys, and eating sweets, and sliding down the banisters and all that. But it is true that when you grow up you don't want to do the same sort of things you did when you were small. Like the boy in Stevenson's poem who says, "When I am grown to man's estate, I shall be very proud and great, and tell the other girls and boys not to meddle with my toys." Getting to heaven, St. Paul indicates, isn't just a thing like going home for the holidays, which makes a

The Gospel in Slow Motion

difference in the circumstances of your life; it's a thing like growing up, which makes a difference in *you*. The Corinthian who had received the gift of prophecy was apt to be very pleased about it, like a child that has been given a new rocking-horse. And St. Paul said, "Very nice, to be sure; but you won't need the rocking-horse when you grow up and have real horses to ride. You won't want the gift of prophecy in heaven because you'll see, you'll know; there will be nothing to prophesy *about*."

And then, as if feeling that he'd been pouring cold water on them a bit too much, he alters his metaphor. The glimpses of knowledge, the glimpses of insight into the future, and into the spiritual world, which we get here, are only glimpses; they aren't a patch on the real thing. Here on earth we're only seeing things in a mirror, as it were—and of course you've got to remember that looking-glasses in St. Paul's time weren't the sort of thing looking-glasses are nowadays; they were only made of metal, and probably not frightfully shiny at that. I should think it was rather like looking at your reflection in a spoon; you know, with your face all drawn-out long-ways, or else bulging in all directions. Even the plainest of you, looking at her reflection in a spoon, can comfort herself with the thought that she's a good deal better-looking than that. And heaven, says St. Paul, is not merely having a *different* kind of knowledge, it's having a much *better* kind of knowledge, which makes all your spiritual gifts look foolish. And St. Paul had been taken up into the third heaven, so perhaps he knew what he was talking about.

After all, he concludes, there are three gifts which *really* matter, which no Christian can do without: faith, hope and charity. And of these, he says, charity is the greatest; it is typical of St. Paul that he forgets to say why. His whole point (but he forgets to mention it) is that charity lasts on in heaven, whereas faith and hope don't. We shall all be hopeless in heaven; we shall all be faithless in heaven. No room for hope, when you've got there; no room for faith, when you can see the things with your own eyes. But charity—this bond of fellowship which unites us to God and unites us to our fellow-creatures—that will go on eternally; it is the atmosphere, the condition of heaven; it *is* heaven.

CHAPTER 18

The Apostle of the Midlands

He that humbles himself shall be exalted. (LUKE 14:11)

I WANT TO PREACH TO YOU THIS AFTERNOON ABOUT St. Chad. We don't often take much interest in St. Chad, perhaps chiefly because he has got such an uninspiring name; it sounds like a kind of fish. But then he lived before the Norman conquest, when as you will know from your history books everybody had rather silly names—they were all called Eggbald or Earwig or something like that. But he is one of the Saints of this diocese; and I thought we would dig him up this afternoon, partly because he is a very nice, gentle kind of Saint, and partly because very little indeed is known about him; so there will be no danger of your having a sermon unsuitably long for half-term. I'm afraid he will bring in a certain amount of history, but I will try to keep history out of the thing as much as possible. Still, you've got to get the setting. He lived round about A.D. 650, four hundred years before the Norman conquest, when England wasn't a single kingdom, but divided up. It was about two hundred years since the Angles, Saxons, and Jutes had come to settle down in these parts, and some of them were only just beginning to turn Christian. Some of them were converted by St. Augustine and his missionaries, who had come over from Rome about fifty years before; others from the north, by missionaries from Ireland. Ireland, you have to remember, was then about the most civilized country in Europe. It lay so far to the west that nobody had ever taken the trouble to invade it, at a time when the whole of Europe and the whole of England were being overrun by barbarians. So in those days you didn't go over to Ireland for the hunting or the fishing or the racing; you went there to get learning. And St. Chad went there to do his studies; but after a bit he was called back to England. He had a brother called Cedd (there were four brothers in that family, all beginning with the letter C. It's confusing for the postman, but some families are like that); St. Cedd (he was a Saint too), had just died at his Abbey of Lastingham, in Yorkshire, not very far from Ampleforth; and when he died, he asked that his brother Chad might be made abbot instead of him. So St. Chad came to Lastingham, and he made such a good abbot that it wasn't long before they wanted to make him a bishop. But here there was a bit of a mix-up. England seems to have been so full of Saints just then that there weren't enough dioceses to go round. And St. Wilfrid (I expect you've heard of St. Wilfrid) and St. Chad were both sent off to get themselves consecrated, each of them to be bishop of Northumbria.

St. Wilfrid was the sort of person who likes to do things properly, and he went off to France to get consecrated. There had been a lot of trouble in England, just then, about the right way of calculating Easter. The missionaries in the north, who as I say came from Ireland, used to celebrate Easter on a different day from the

The Gospel in Slow Motion

whole of the rest of Europe. Irish people are like that, sometimes; they were perfectly good Catholics, but they had their own ways of doing things. Well, I don't know why they all got so hot and bothered about the right date for keeping Easter, but they did; and St. Wilfrid, who was very strong on doing everything in the Roman way, because after all if you were going to be a Catholic you had got to follow Rome's lead, went off to France so as to make quite sure he was being consecrated by bishops who were quite sound about the right date for keeping Easter. St. Chad, I should think, didn't mind much about that sort of thing. He was quite sound on the great Easter question himself, but he didn't *bother*. So he went off to Canterbury to get consecrated; and when he found that the archbishop there had just died, he wandered off into Sussex and collected some bishops there and got himself consecrated, without asking them what date they kept Easter. And the result was that he got in ahead of St. Wilfrid, and when St. Wilfrid got back from France he found that his see was already occupied. However, he was a Saint too; so he didn't make a fuss like people do when their seats are taken in railway trains; he just went off to Ripon and looked after his abbey there, quite happy.

I should think he was probably more happy than St. Chad; I doubt if St. Chad ever got much fun out of being a bishop. But he was an awfully good bishop. He used to wander all round the countryside on foot, always on foot, preaching in all the towns and villages and getting people to come and be baptized. That was all right, but a year or two later a new Archbishop of Canterbury arrived from Rome, called St. Theodore. He was a holy man too, but he was one of those people who can't leave things alone; one of those efficient people whom Rome is always sending out to try and tighten things up. I've no doubt they were perfectly right; the Church in England had obviously got into a very untidy state with all these Angles and Saxons and Jutes settling down all over the place and having to be converted from heathenism, and I don't suppose that keeping Easter on the wrong day was the only eccentric thing about English Christianity. The Popes, after all, were trying to tidy up the whole of Europe; it wasn't just England that was all anyhow; the barbarians coming in from the east and north had disturbed all the landmarks of Europe, and the Popes then had as hard a job to keep things going properly as Pope Pius XII does. By the way, tomorrow isn't only St. Chad's day, it's the anniversary of the Holy Father's election; so will you all please say a prayer for his intentions? Well, as I was saying, it was probably a good thing to have a tidy up, but it made trouble in Northumbria.

From St. Theodore's point of view, St. Chad was all wrong, because the bishops who had consecrated him hadn't been officially reconciled to the true date for keeping Easter. And St. Wilfrid, who was quite happy managing his abbey at Ripon, was the real bishop. So St. Theodore told St. Chad he was very sorry, but he was afraid St. Chad would have to clear out. And then he no doubt waited for an explosion of anger and a mule-like obstinacy on St. Chad's part, because I expect they'd warned him in Rome that these English were a tough sort of people to deal with. Instead of which, St. Chad said, "Well, as a matter of fact I never wanted to take on the job at all; I never felt worthy of it. So if you really think I haven't been properly consecrated, that's splendid; I can go back to Lastingham." I need hardly say that St. Theodore took that well. St. Wilfrid

The Gospel in Slow Motion

was put into his see; but a year or two later, when King Wulfhere of Mercia asked to have a bishop consecrated for his kingdom, St. Theodore gave him St. Chad. And that is why St. Chad belongs to us in the Midlands, although all his early work for the Faith was done in the north, where they have quite enough Saints to keep them going already.

St. Chad fixed his cathedral at Lichfield; he thought it ought to be a holy place because there was a legend that a thousand British Christians had been massacred there long before by the Romans; I believe the place where it is supposed to have happened is still called Heavenfield. I've no doubt that he still had to travel round a good deal, because his new diocese extended from the banks of the Severn here to the Lincolnshire coast. By the way, when St. Theodore sent him to Mercia he warned him that it was rather a waste of time going round on foot—"you ought to ride a horse, like me"; and when St. Chad began to explain how he thought it was more apostolic to go round on foot, St. Theodore, always efficient, just heaved him onto the horse, which was standing by, and made him ride it. What the horse did, I don't know, but I suppose St. Chad must have consented to save time by doing some of his business on horseback. When he was at Lichfield, he didn't live in a palace; he built himself a kind of priory where he lived with seven or eight monks; he didn't want to stop being a monk just because he was a bishop.

I wish we knew more about him. One thing we are told about him is a curious attitude he had towards the weather. If the wind blew strong, he went down on his knees and prayed for mercy. If it turned into a real storm, especially a thunderstorm, he went on praying and saying psalms till the weather cleared up again. It wasn't that he was frightened, but, you see, he felt he ought to be frightened. Because these violent upheavals of nature, he explained, were a warning God sends us to show how great his power is, and what respect we ought to have for him. The longest story that is preserved about him I'm afraid probably isn't true; St. Bede doesn't mention it, and it doesn't give a very plausible account of King Wulfhere, who seems to have been a perfectly good Christian. But the story is that Wulfhere had promised to bring up his children as Christians and didn't. And then one of his sons was hunting a stag, and the stag burst in to where St. Chad was, and took refuge in a stream. St. Chad tied a cord round its neck and turned it loose in the forest. The young prince turned up after a time, and didn't ask, "Are you the missing person?"; he asked, "Have you see the missing stag?" And St. Chad proceeded to preach him a sermon about the hart desiring the water-brooks, which he said was a type of baptism. And it was funny, he said, what a lot there is about birds and beasts in the Bible; look at that dove which came back to the Ark—that was a type of baptism too. And the prince, who was getting bored, said, "I'll believe in baptism if you can make that stag come back here by praying about it." Well, that was a silly thing to say, because of course St. Chad fell on his knees and the stag wandered in with cord round its neck almost at once. And the prince was baptized, and so, afterwards, was his brother. And their father, King Wulfhere, was so angry that he killed them both; which is where the story gets improbable.

King Wulfhere, the story goes on, repented of what he'd done, and set out to find St. Chad and get absolution. St. Chad was saying Mass, and when Wulfhere looked in through the window of the

The Gospel in Slow Motion

chapel, he found it all full of a heavenly light that made the sunshine look silly. When Mass was over, he went in, and asked to see St. Chad, and St. Chad was so hot and bothered by the thought of having to absolve a king from murder before breakfast that when he took off his vestments he hung them up on a sunbeam by mistake. It was the sort of absentminded thing, I imagine, he would do; but the odd thing according to the story is that the vestments hung there all right. That disposed of any doubts Wulfhere may have had, and he made his confession at once. I wish that story was true, because I don't know any other instance of a saint hanging anything up, successfully, on a sunbeam.

An epidemic broke out at Lichfield, and St. Chad fell ill. A monk, working in the garden near where he lay, heard a noise of singing, up in the sky, that seemed to come nearer and nearer, till it got to the room where St. Chad was, and then mount slowly into the sky once more. Just then, a window was thrown open, and St. Chad called to him to summon all the monks to his bedside. He explained that he had only a week to live, and gave the monks some final directions. He admitted, afterwards, that the voices from the sky had told him about it; and a week later he died.

They buried him at Lichfield, and he had a beautiful shrine in its beautiful cathedral later on. There he lay till the Reformation; and at the Reformation a curious thing happened. The shrine wasn't looted, but the body disappeared. It was many years later that it was found, in the keeping of a pious Catholic; he and his family were quite poor people, who had kept the faith, and had kept the body of the Saint, which had been entrusted to them to save it from the possibility of outrage at the hands of the Protestant mob. It was then given into the keeping of a well-known Catholic family—I shan't tell you the name of the family—and they had it till the Catholic Cathedral at Birmingham was built, and was dedicated to St. Chad. If you are going to Birmingham from here by G.W.R., look out to your left just as you get into Snowhill Station, and you will see a large brick building with two spires standing up rather like the ears of a rabbit. That is St. Chad's cathedral; and that is where St. Chad is now, all that was mortal of him.

I haven't left myself any time to draw a moral. But if I've succeeded in giving you any hint of the Saint's atmosphere, that will be better than any moral. It enriches our English countryside, to think how many of the roads, in all probability, have been trodden by the feet of patient missionaries like St. Chad, all those centuries ago. He doesn't quite belong to us; it was some years after his death that Shropshire became part of the kingdom of Mercia; about the same time that St. Milburg, whose feast came last Monday, started the abbey at Wenlock. But I daresay he looked at us across the Severn (perhaps riding the horse St. Theodore shoved him onto), and wished there were a bridge at Bridgnorth. May his prayers, with the prayers of our Blessed Lady and all the Saints, be with us in times not less troubled than his, and win safety and peace for the country which he loved, for the country which he loves.

CHAPTER 19

An Uncomfortable Saint

Sell what you have, and give alms, so providing yourselves with purses that time cannot wear holes in, an inexhaustible treasure laid up in heaven. (LUKE 12:33)

I DON'T THINK THIS IS ONE OF THE PASSAGES IN WHICH our present translation is very happy in its rendering; "Make to yourselves bags which grow not old" sounds rather silly, somehow. I want to preach to you about St. Peter of Alcantara. He was a Spaniard; and the reason why we are making a fuss of him is because our cathedral at Shrewsbury is dedicated to him; and why that is, I don't know. But there is no harm in your knowing a bit more about St. Peter of Alcantara. He is remembered for two things especially. He was born just at the threshold of the sixteenth century, the century of the Protestant Reformation. And, as perhaps you know, it was also a century of Catholic Reformation. The whole Church, between 1500 and 1650, was dusted up and spring-cleaned. New religious orders, the Jesuits especially, came into being and put new life into things. But what was perhaps still more important, the old religious orders began to reform themselves. They had gone slack, in varying degrees, and become worldly; some quite pious people, in despair, wondered whether they oughtn't to be liquidated altogether. And then, in this marvellous period which we call the period of the Counter-reformation, men and women were found in the religious orders who saw that this wasn't good enough, and not only began to live a much stricter life themselves, but induced their fellow-religious to do the same. That, believe me, was a tough job. Well, St. Peter was a Franciscan, and started, in Spain and Portugal, a whole province of Franciscans who went back to the strict observance of St. Francis' rule, and in some ways made it even stricter than it had been. That is one achievement which made him famous.

But perhaps he is still better known as the friend and counsellor of St. Teresa—not St. Thérèse of Lisieux, who lived four centuries later, but the great mystic, St. Teresa of Ávila. She, with his advice, reformed the Carmelite order as he had reformed the Franciscans. And it was very largely due to St. Peter that St. Teresa ever became known for the Saint she was. People used to think she must be a bit weak in the head, having all these visions and these extraordinary ways of prayer, until St. Peter got to know her and convinced everybody, including the bishop—it's very hard, as a rule, to convince bishops of anything—that St. Teresa's spirit was all right, and came from God.

Meanwhile, St. Peter's own life is an extraordinary document in many ways. He is extraordinary, even among the favoured Saints of that amazing century, for his ecstasies, and for the levitation which accompanied them. He seems to have made a habit of wandering out into lonely fields to say his prayers, because he felt sure he would have an ecstasy, and be lifted up in the air, and he hated being watched. He really seems to have had no control over himself when he was saying his prayers. "In the jubilation of his soul," we read in Alban Butler's *Lives of the Saints*, "...he was not able to contain himself from singing the divine praises aloud in a wonderful manner." That is all very well, but it is not what his biographer says. His biographer says that "he uttered noises so terrifying, that the brethren were panic-stricken whenever they heard them." That is hardly the way in which one describes singing, even when the singing is very bad. No, I suppose that the saint uttered loud groans, just because he couldn't help himself; he didn't know what he was doing, and the brethren had to make the best of it. But I'm not going to preach to you about all that, because I think it is the sort of thing which produces curiosity, rather than edification.

And again, St. Peter was distinguished even among the Spanish saints, who treated themselves with great brutality, by the penances which he undertook, the scourgings and the hair-shirts and the spikes he wore next his skin, and so on. I am sure you are all longing to hear about that; you probably like a story with plenty of blood in it. But I'm not going to dwell on mortifications either; at least, not on that kind of mortification. You see, spikes and hair-shirts and things are a way of offering satisfaction for one's own sins, and for other people's. But there are other mortifications, like living very hard, eating and sleeping very little, which both do that and at the same time do something to our character, they make us less dependent on creature comforts, more grateful to God for his simple gifts, more free for saying our prayers. That is why St. Francis was keen that his friars should live a hard life; he wanted them to be free, free from the entanglements of the world. And that was,

RONALD KNOX

in the main, why St. Peter was so keen on tightening up the discipline of the Order. He said as much to St. Teresa, when St. Teresa was worrying whether she should adopt hundred percent poverty as the rule of Carmel. "The care," he told her, "which is required for administering temporal revenues turns the mind from heavenly things." In his own order, he insisted that the brethren should really live by begging, and starve if necessary; anything was better than having to keep accounts.

And he wasn't gentle with them. They never ate meat or fish or eggs, they always went barefoot, they slept on boards, and with very little room to live in. When he built a house for eight friars, he would make it thirty-two feet long and twenty-eight feet wide; that included the church, and the whole thing would work out about the size of this chapel, or rather less. The church was only eight feet wide, with a high altar and a Lady altar, no more. Your bed took up exactly half of your bedroom; the cloister was so small that if you stood at one end you could touch hands with a friar standing at the other end. St. Peter was dominated, I think, with the idea that you should make do with the absolute bare minimum; in your bedroom you must have room to undress and room to sleep, but not more; in the cloister there must be enough room for eight friars to assemble before meals, but there was no reason why there should be room to walk about. This preoccupation of his seems to find its way even into his miracles. Once, when he was on a journey, his companion was fainting for hunger; St. Peter told him to go and look under a particular bush, and what do you think he found there? A newly-baked loaf of bread, and one sardine. Not overdoing the thing, you see; St. Peter of course wouldn't have touched

The Gospel in Slow Motion

fish, but as a special concession to his long fast, the brother might have one sardine.

I need hardly say that St. Peter himself lived the roughest of any. He slept for an hour and half out of the twenty-four, and took a meal once in three days—he was surprised that St. Teresa hadn't noticed what a convenient arrangement that was. He only ate black bread; on festivals he allowed himself some half-cooked vegetables. When he went out to dine, as he often had to, in grand houses, he started by saying that his digestion was so bad, he was afraid he could only manage a plate of soup—I dare say it was true, by that time; and when he'd tasted it he would make a face and say, "Excuse me, this soup is so hot, may I put a little cold water in it?" Then he would douche it with cold water till it tasted of nothing at all. He never wore a hat, in sun, rain or snow, because he thought it wouldn't be respected to wear a hat in the presence of God, and he always lived in the presence of God. He only had one habit to wear. Once a Dominican called and was told he was in the garden; he went there and found St. Peter apparently sun-bathing, with hardly anything on. And he looked rather shocked, but St. Peter explained that he had been washing his habit; our Lord had said he was only to have one, and he couldn't put it on till it had finished drying on a bush. His favourite cell was four feet long and three feet wide, and it was too low for him to stand up straight in it; he slept and prayed there, and did everything else in the garden, which was ten feet by five. Always just the minimum, you see; the less you had, the less creatures would mean to you. His friars didn't even possess their tiny little house; it was built for them by a patron, and every year they had to go and give him back the keys, and thank him for making them so comfortable all this year; and would he, out of charity, lend it them for one year more? It doesn't sound a very comfortable life, does it? But St. Peter didn't just found one friary, he founded a whole province of friaries, all over Spain and Portugal, all living by this curiously narrow rule.

Well, how are we going to get a lesson out of all that? I think the lesson St. Peter meant it to teach—he lived, remember, in an age when Spain had become very luxurious indeed—was that we all ought to accustom ourselves to do with a little less than we can take if we want to, so as to keep ourselves free, untrammelled; so as not to let the flesh get the better of the spirit. Eat what's put before you, but go slow about the second helping, especially when there is competition for it; sleep in your nice bed, but be careful of that extra five minutes which is so tempting, and yet just throws out the programme of your work or your prayer; have the run of your nice big rooms, but don't throw things about all over the place just anyhow, because that will come to mean that you can't do without a big room to live in. That's what I think he would say to you and me; we must be free, we mustn't let our comforts dominate us. It's practical advice, too, in these times; most of you will probably marry someone who's quite poor, and it will be a pity if by then you have come to depend on your comforts. It is going to turn you into a grumpy, unspiritual sort of person.

Like all people who, for the love of God, deny themselves everything except the barest necessities, St. Peter had a blind trust in Providence. I told you the miracle of the sardine; that sort of thing was always happening. The friary is snowed up, there is no food left in the place; then, a ring at the bell, a couple of big baskets

The Gospel in Slow Motion

full of food are shoved in at the front door as it opens, and when the brethren look outside, there is nobody there, and there are no marks in the snow. That sort of story sounds incredible when it happened four hundred years ago. And yet, it used to happen in the life of St. John Bosco, who only died in the year I was born. The Cardinal Bourne told me he had talked to one of St. John Bosco's first companions; and he said that miracles which helped to fill the larder were so common in the house at Turin that you hardly noticed them. Perhaps you find that incredible too; but, believe me, Providence doesn't let you down, if you manage to cut your schedule of requirements in life pretty low. So let's learn that, too, from St. Peter; a strong trust in Providence.

Another quality went with, and sprang from, St. Peter's love of self-denial; he was always recollected; you may say he was always at prayer. He went about with his eyes fixed on the ground, and as a rule he kept them shut. More than once, it seems, he walked across a river in full flood, and was quite surprised afterwards when people reminded him that there wasn't a bridge. On the other hand, it meant that he was always rather bother-headed about finding his way anywhere; and it is solemnly put down among his bodily mortifications that he was always hitting his head against the ceiling; which isn't remarkable considering how low the ceilings were, and that he was never on the lookout for them. Well, I'm not suggesting that you should try to cross the Severn, or even the Mor Brook, without finding a bridge; and I'm not suggesting that you should go about all the time with your eyes shut, because although you might not hit your heads you would be always running into people. But I do want you to consider whether we might not, all of us, try to be a bit more recollected than we are; try to think, sometimes, about God's presence with us as we go about our daily lives, and lift up our hearts in gratitude and love to him.

Our Blessed Lord said to St. Teresa, in a vision, "The merits of Brother Peter of Alcantara are so eminent, and have such weight with me, that whatever is asked in his name, I will never refuse." That is worth thinking of, because St. Teresa generally knew what she was talking about. So shall we ask St. Peter to get for us, besides any other gifts he sees us to be specially in need of, some faint echo of his spirit of poverty, his spirit of trust in Providence, his spirit of recollection? If we do that, perhaps we shall learn to be grateful to the people who built Shrewsbury cathedral, for obliging us to think about him on this anniversary of his death.

CHAPTER 20

The Lump

Then he put before them another parable. The kingdom of heaven, he said, is like a grain of mustard seed, that a man has taken and sowed in his ground; of all seeds, none is so little, but when it grows up it is greater than any garden herb; it grows into a tree, so that all the birds come and settle in its branches. And he told them still another parable, The kingdom of heaven is like leaven, that a woman has taken and buried away in three measures of meal, enough to leaven the whole batch. All this Jesus said to the multitude in parables, and would say it in parables only, so fulfilling the words which were spoken by the prophet, I will speak my mind in parables, I will give utterance to things which have been kept secret from the beginning of the world. (MATT. 13:31–35)

CARDINAL NEWMAN, SOMEWHERE IN HIS WORKS, GIVES A description of what one means by a gentleman. One point in it, I know, is this, "His eyes are on all his company"; that's a very good rule to adopt in life if you want to have good manners—never forget about anybody who's in the room; don't talk above the heads of the children, don't neglect the elderly just because talking to them means shouting to them. I'm afraid that we preachers are apt to be rather careless about this excellent prescription; and one thing we always do—when we single out an imaginary member of our audience it is always a man; we always forget that there are women in church. The preacher who never forgot about that was our Lord. Women used to come and listen to him preaching, so he was very careful not to be above their heads. When he was talking about the coming destruction of Jerusalem, he used the words, "Two men will be working in the field, one will be taken and the other left." And then, you see, he added, "Two women shall be grinding at the mill, one shall be taken and the other left"; he doesn't forget about the women. Or again, he asks, "If a man has a hundred sheep and loses one, doesn't he search for it all day and rejoice when it is found?" And then immediately he adds, "Or suppose it's a woman, who has only gotten pennies in the house, if she loses one, what a fuss there is about it!" Perhaps it may have happened to our Lady, I don't know, but my point is that the women don't get left out in our Lord's preaching. And so here; the kingdom of heaven is like a man planting a mustard seed, true enough; but don't forget it's also exactly like a woman putting leaven into a lump of dough any time she is baking, so you women at the back must listen just the same.

The point of the mustard seed is that it is very small—that's why our Lord talks elsewhere about having faith the size of a grain of mustard seed, and yet once it's planted it grows up in a very short space of time; grows up, not quite into what we should call a tree, but into a large shrub, quite large enough for birds to come and swing themselves on the branches. And the point of leaven, only I think one ordinarily uses something called baking-powder

The Gospel in Slow Motion

nowadays, is that if you forget to put it in when you bake you never get your bread or your cake but only a solid lump of dough; whereas if you put in some leaven, it doesn't matter where, it will spread in no time, and the bread will rise as it's meant to. I dare say some of you are allowed to play at cooking at home; if so you know more about it than I do. But our Lord's parables only expect you to get just the rough hang of the situation. It's nice to think, isn't it, that when he preached like this, he was going back to his boyhood and the odd bits of knowledge he had picked up by asking questions. You can see St. Joseph in the garden, and our Lord saying, "What a tiny seed that is"; and, "How long will it take to grow?" and, "How big will it be when it does grow?" just like any other boy of his age. You can see our Lady baking, and our Lord standing by and saying, "Mother, what is that curious thing? And why do you only put in such a little of it?"; and, "What is the use of putting it in?"; and, "What would happen if you didn't put it in?"—and she would remember all that later on, when she stood there and heard him preaching to the crowds.

Well, what was the point he was getting at in these two parables? He was talking about the kingdom of heaven, the reign of God on earth, by which he always means his Church. The people who were listening to him were looking forward to the coming of *a* kingdom of heaven; but they had got it all wrong; they thought that God would suddenly manifest his power and come down to redress all wrongs and put everything straight, and then there would be a millennium, a reign of universal peace and prosperity, with the Jews lording it over the Gentiles instead of the Gentiles lording it over the Jews. And in most of his parables our Lord is telling them, or hinting to them, that they are wrong. So it is here. It's quite true, he says, that the kingdom of God will come very quickly, but it won't come in a thunderclap; it has got to grow, just as things in nature grow, by a silent, secret process. You can't watch the mustard seed growing, you can't watch the leaven at work, but you know they are there, and because they are there they are bound to take their effect. Before people know where they are, this kingdom of mine, my Church, will have grown up mysteriously everywhere, and this gospel of mine will be infecting men's minds, spreading its influence in spite of all attempts to stop it.

You will notice that the two parables are not quite the same. The mustard tree grows by taking something from its surroundings; the soil nourishes it, the rain waters it, the sun fosters it; and it grows visibly from day to day; you can put a stick down beside it and check its height every morning. Whereas the leaven doesn't grow; nor does it take anything away from its surroundings; on the contrary, it communicates something to its surroundings; it gives, it radiates life *to* other things instead of taking life to itself *from* other things; in that sense, the leaven is just the opposite of the mustard seed. How, then, can the kingdom of heaven be like both at once?

The fact is, that it *is* like both at once. It all depends on the angle from which you look at the thing. The Church does grow, like the mustard seed, does grow rapidly, like the mustard seed, does grow secretly, like the mustard seed; and, like the mustard seed, in the process of growing it takes away something from its surroundings. It adds to its own numbers, taking men away from the worship of false gods, leaving the temples of the heathen empty. And it grows with the splendid unity of organic life; the Church today, with its hundreds of millions of souls, is the same thing as that mustard seed, that tiny body of a hundred and twenty friends of the risen Christ, who waited in the cenacle for the Holy Ghost to come down on them at the day of Pentecost. But if you look at it from another point of view, you will see that our Lord didn't merely leave behind him a body of people to represent him. He left behind him in the world an influence, an infectious influence, which has penetrated and permeated the world ever since. Or, if you care to alter the metaphor a little, he has left behind him a spark, which has caught here and caught there, died down here and come to life again there, as it was fanned by the wind of grace, from the day of Pentecost to this. Only, whereas the Church is a visible body, whose numbers you can count up by taking a census of them, just like that mustard tree we used to go and measure every morning after breakfast, this influence which Christ left behind him in the world is like the leaven; it works secretly; there is no means of gauging its strength or of calculating its movements; where it will die down, where it will break out afresh. The mustard tree, growing high and spreading wide for all the world to see, the leaven, burrowing away secretly in the dead lump of humanity and passing on its infectious influence—either comparison will serve, if we want to give an account of the difference there's been in the world, since Christ came to us.

Now, there's a great deal to be said about the growth of the mustard tree. It is fascinating to watch the history of the Christian Church through the centuries, its defeats and its triumphs, its deaths and its resurrections. I suppose, when our Lord spoke of the mustard tree, he was thinking in the first instance of the almost miraculous way in which the Church spread from end to end of the civilized world, when the whole force of the Roman Empire was determined to crush it, and of its triumph under Constantine. But, you see, I don't want to give you a lecture in history. And besides, I don't think that side of the picture is the one to dwell on in a sermon; it doesn't point out any lesson to us about what we ought to be doing, what we ought to be avoiding. The growth of the Church is something that happens under the influence of God's grace, with no visible relation to the efforts man makes to propagate its doctrines. You and I can't make converts; God makes converts. No, the growth of the Church, whether in its numbers or in its influence, is something that we can worry about, something that we can pray about, something that we can thank God about; and we can help foreign missions and all sorts of good works in the hope that God will use these means to bring souls to himself. But we're only preparing the way for the growth of the Church when we do that; "I planted," St. Paul says, "and Apollo watered, but it is God who gave the increase no human soul can, in the strict sense, convert another human soul."

But, in the matter of the leaven, it's different. You see, it's the nature of leaven that everything which it influences passes on that influence to something else. If you don't see what I mean, take a very simple instance. If you take an ordinary piece of bread, such as you have for your tea, and leave it close to one of the altar-breads in the sacristy, you'll find that in a few minutes the altar-bread begins to shrivel up and curl at the edges. Why's that? Because it's unleavened bread, and it can't stay close to ordinary leavened bread without being affected by its influence. And that is what is happening to us human beings all the time. We are being affected by one another's

The Gospel in Slow Motion

influence. It may be for the good, it may be for the bad. Our Lord compared his own kingdom, the influence of his own gospel, to leaven; but he also told his apostles to beware of the leaven of the Pharisees and Sadducees, the infectious influence of their false doctrine, and St. Paul tells us to get rid of the leaven of malice and wickedness. We are influencing one another all the time, then, for good or evil. Those of us who have plenty of vitality, plenty of character, are passing on our influence, good or bad, to the others, to the lump. And that good or evil influence that we have passes on; passes on, from life to life, beyond our control, like ripples on the water. Each of you is growing up to be either good leaven in the world around her, or bad leaven, or just part of the lump. And here, where you all live so close together and exchange your opinions and copy one another such a lot, that leavening process, though on a very small scale, has already started.

The bad leaven—it's awfully easy to be bad leaven, you know. Take the habit of grumbling; see how that spreads; one person starts picking holes, and in a day or two everybody else is picking holes too; nothing but grievances where there wasn't any grievance before. Take the habit of uncharitable criticism; how short a time it takes for one sharp tongue to ruin the peace of a whole crowd of people living together, just by starting a fashion of uncharitable speech. Or take the habit of laughing at piety; how easy it is to make everybody round you shy and self-conscious about their religion and almost afraid of saying their prayers! The leaven of malice and wickedness! Anybody who is like that here is doing quite a lot of harm in a small way, with limited opportunities; she will do a great deal more harm in the world before she's finished.

RONALD KNOX

More probably, you are just part of the lump—the herd of people that doesn't set examples, but follows them. You take your colour from your surroundings; what you will make of life depends a great deal on the crowd of people you find yourself thrown in with, on the husband you marry, if you do marry, on the tone of society in general, by the time you are out in it, whatever that may be—(pretty loathsome, if it's anything like what happened after the last war.) If you feel that that's your class, that there's more lump than leaven about you, let me just say this. You mustn't think you aren't having any effect on your world. No, the leavened lump carries the leaven, and the infection of the bad influence other people have on you will spread from you to other people, though it may be without your knowing it, without your fully realizing it. So, if you are that kind of person, do try to develop a little of what the Americans call sales-resistance; do learn to fade out unobtrusively when there's grumbling going on, or uncharitable talk, or anything else that poisons the springs of character. And do learn to pick your friends. The way to pick your friends is not to ask yourself, "Do I like So-and-so," but to ask yourself, "Would I like to be like So-and-so?" If not, So-and-so is no friend for you.

And then some of you, I hope, are being, some of you, I hope, will be, the good leaven. The little society in which you move here is, without knowing it, the sweeter for your passing; later on, your influence will perhaps carry further, and have less transitory effects. Well, I don't want to give you any moral advice, if you feel you want to be that sort of person, because moral advice might only turn you into a prig; and it isn't the plaster angels that do the good in this world. No, I'll only say this, that if you want to have good leaven to communicate to the world, that good leaven must be communicated to you, by divine grace. It is in the Holy Eucharist above all that this gift will come to you; through regular reception of it, even when you are not feeling in the mood for devotion; by offering yourself up to God in and through and with the presence of Jesus Christ in your soul, when you make your thanksgiving, steadily and self-abandoningly, even when you aren't conscious of any sweetness or consolation, but only of distractions and a desire to fidget. The unleavened Bread of sincerity and truth—it is this unleavened Bread from heaven that will communicate to us, miraculously if you like, but everything about it is miraculous, that leaven with which we, Christ's followers, ought to be leavening the earth. Till the whole was leavened; it will be a long time before that happens to this world of ours; but the leavening process is going on all the time, and it is one in which we can all take a share, all do take a share, for good or evil, whether we want it or not.

CHAPTER 21

Ups and Downs

I know what it is to be brought low, and what it is to have abundance of everything; I have been apprenticed to everything, having my fill and going hungry, living in plenty and living in want; nothing is beyond my powers, thanks to the strength God gives me. (PHIL. 4:12)

I THOUGHT THIS WOULD BE A USEFUL TEXT FROM WHICH to preach to you about St. Elizabeth of Hungary. I don't know whether that will be a very popular subject; not many of you are called Elizabeth, and not very large ones, but anyhow you have a good deal to learn from her.

She was born in 1207, which as you all know was eight years before King John signed the Magna Carta. What is more important is that it was just about the time when St. Francis of Assisi was turned out of doors by his father and started on his career as a Saint. St. Elizabeth lived her whole life, you may say, in the Franciscan spirit, and died a Franciscan tertiary; she was responsible, indeed, for bringing the Franciscans into Germany at all. But she and St. Francis never met. At the age of four, she got engaged to be married. It wasn't usual, in those days, to consult the bride and bridegroom about whether they wanted to marry or not; so St. Elizabeth was knocked down to a boy of almost her own age, who was going, later on, to be duke of Hesse. What seems still more extraordinary, and I don't think it was usual even in those days, she left at the age of four her own home, the royal court of Hungary, and went to live in Germany, with the family of her future husband. I suppose they felt that it was never too soon to make the acquaintance of your relations-in-law; so much depends, after all, on getting on well with them. As a matter of fact, they must have thought pretty well of her, because when her fiancé died—she was nine years old at the time—they didn't treat it as all off; they said she would do for the next brother, Louis, who was now the heir to the dukedom. So she stayed on with the Hesse family in their great castle, the Wartburg. It was in the same castle, about three hundred years later, that Martin Luther took refuge, when he started to be a heretic and didn't like the idea of being a martyr; he lived shut up in the Wartburg and spent his time translating the New Testament.

However, let's go back to St. Elizabeth. She didn't really fit in very well, all the same. You see, at that time the court of Hesse was the high spot in European social life, and a tremendous place for troubadours and all that sort of thing; money flowed freely. But St. Elizabeth from her earliest years could never see any use for money except to give it away. She spent her whole time giving away the pocket-money which was sent her from Hungary, and making clothes for the starving children, and so on; and it got her no good marks with her relations-in-law. There was a famous occasion when she and her future sister-in-law were taken to church for some State function and made to wear gold coronets, which must have been very uncomfortable. St. Elizabeth wouldn't have minded about hers being uncomfortable, but she was found kneeling in floods of tears before a crucifix, with her coronet off because, she said, she couldn't bear to wear a gold coronet in the presence of her Saviour crowned with thorns. Whether she had a beret to put on instead the story doesn't tell us. But I don't know whether they were so particular in those parts about having your head covered in church; in Yugoslavia even now the women don't seem to bother about it at all. Incidentally, what St. Paul says is that a woman shouldn't pray or prophesy with her head uncovered; he doesn't say that if she leaves her rosary in chapel and wants to go and retrieve it she must put on a beret before she goes in. Still more incidentally, talking about chapel reminds me of it; I am always meaning to tell you about something which you do wrong in chapel, and will all those who are not listening please listen. No, it's not about fainting. There are about half a dozen of you who *will* not keep their heads up when they go to Communion; and that makes it impossible for me, in the pitch darkness which we get this side of the altar step, to see where their mouths are. So will you please all be careful to hold your heads well up.

But let's go back to St. Elizabeth. That story didn't do her any good with her future mother-in-law; though I'm bound to say some people will tell you that this lady, the Duchess Sophia, was rather a pious creature really, and she hadn't much to do with bullying St. Elizabeth, though bullied St. Elizabeth undoubtedly was. But the time came when her future husband, Louis, left school, and when he came back home the great question was whether they were going to marry or not. The Duchess Sophia, whether from the best or from the worst motives, said here *is* this girl and we've arranged for her to marry you, but really I don't know whether it would be a very good plan; she seems much more suited to be a nun. And here comes the curious part of the story. You were expecting, weren't you, that her husband would turn out to be a horrible, brutal man who would ill-treat her for years, and then get rather unfairly converted on his death-bed. Not a bit of it; the young Louis seems to have been a person of excellent dispositions, and is regarded in Germany as a saint. No doubt he wasn't up to her standard, but he was very keen on the idea of marrying her—perhaps he was in love with her—and said he thought all this idea of giving money away to the poor and dressing in woolen clothes which weren't even dyed was just the right thing. And they married and lived happily for some time after.

Very happily, I think you can say. The little girl who had been whisked away from home at the age of four, and misunderstood, and laughed at, was now duchess of Hesse (her father-in-law had died) with any amount of money to give away, married and in love with her husband, the mother, as time went on, of three children. Her husband wasn't quite as pious as she was; but she used to kneel most of the night at his bedside saying her prayers and holding his hand in hers, while he went to sleep; which is a pretty picture and no doubt seemed to both of them a fair division of labour. She had a field day when he had to go abroad for a bit one year, spending practically all the ducal revenues on the poor and founding a large hospital in his absence, but he said it was perfectly all right when he came back; I strongly suspect he must have been in love with her. "But then," you say, "what about that story of the roses?" I can

The Gospel in Slow Motion

never make out that story of the roses. In my copy of Butler's *Lives of the Saints* she is represented with her lap full of roses and a large cottage loaf hidden in one hand behind her back. But in the *Breviary*—and the *Breviary* ought to know—the same story is told of her great-niece, St. Elizabeth of Portugal, who was quite a different person. Well, of course, one's great-niece always is a different person, but what I mean is that St. Elizabeth of Portugal was married to a very unpleasant husband, and the story really suits her much better. So let's leave it out, and go back to St. Elizabeth of *Hungary*.

They hadn't been married very many years, in fact it was just before her third baby was born, when Louis was sitting by her bedside one day, and she said how awful it was to think of all the women there were having babies when they were dreadfully poor, and couldn't we do something about it, Louis?—and then, more or less in fun, she opened his purse to take some money off him, and in the purse she found a little red cross. And she knew what that meant; it meant that he had taken a vow to go and fight in the Crusade that was going on at the moment. And he had to admit it, and then there were floods of tears, because St. Elizabeth wasn't one of those saints who never seem to mind about what happens to other people; she was just desperately and furiously unhappy. But it was all right; she soon said, "Not my will, Lord, but thine be done." And Louis went away, and died of a fever in Italy, before he had even embarked for the Holy Land.

This part of the story isn't so jolly, is it? But it gets worse. According to the traditional way of telling it, St. Elizabeth's relations-in-law all turned against her; her brother-in-law decided that *he* would be the new duke of Hesse, instead of her son, and she was turned out, with her three children, into the snow. Some people nowadays will tell you that that is not true, that she left the castle of her own accord. I dare say her own temperament had something to do with it; she was the sort of person who never tried to stick up for her rights—"if she affirmed or denied anything," her biographer tells us, "her words seemed to imply a fear of some mistake." Very likely she welcomed this opportunity of retiring from the world, although for some time she could find nowhere at all to live; and when her husband's body had been brought home and buried, and her little son had been confirmed in his title to the dukedom, she left all the children in the care of her aunt, who was an abbess, and went off to be a Franciscan tertiary, living in a little house with a few of her maids, and devoting herself entirely to the poor.

Probably you can say she was happy again, though it seems to us a bit of a comedown. She didn't really have good luck, even now. Her director was a very curious person called Conrad of Marburg, and I should think he was easily the best-hated person in Europe. He was a most ferocious inquisitor; and it was a letter of his to the Pope which did more than anything else to start that business of hunting out and executing witches that lasted on, in England and Scotland, right up to the end of the seventeenth century. No doubt there is a lot to be said for him and against him, but in any case he was an unpleasantly strict director; and even made St. Elizabeth give notice to her two favourite maids, which very few directors would have the courage to do nowadays. But it didn't make much difference, because St. Elizabeth's cottage life didn't last long—only four years. She died at the age of twenty-four.

The Gospel in Slow Motion

At the age of twenty-four—she had seen a good deal of life, hadn't she, in that time? And she was like St. Paul; she knew what it was to be brought low, and what it was to have abundant means; she had been apprenticed to everything, having her fill and going hungry, living in plenty and living in want; nothing was beyond her powers, thanks to the strength God gave her. I want you to see that sanctity doesn't necessarily depend on being a nun when you grow up. It *is* possible to marry, and to be desperately happy with one's husband and children, and to lose all that, and still to be desperately happy, and to be a Saint, if, but only if, you've got the right angle on life and know what really matters and what doesn't. That charity towards the poor and the sick, by which St. Elizabeth of Hungary is chiefly remembered, wasn't just a rich woman's dodge for filling in time when she was bored. She had realized ever since she could remember that the only way to make yourself happy and keep yourself from brooding, when you were a little girl of four or five living permanently away from your home, was to live not for yourself but for other people. Whatever came along, she could always make do; it was like our Blessed Lady again at Bethlehem, saying what a splendid cradle that Crib makes. And I want *you* to have resources in yourself; not to depend on outside things, rank or money or the love of other people, to keep you happy. If you've only got the love of God which puts first things first, which can see in everything that happens, joys or sorrows as the world calls them, the material for letting you do his will and letting his will be done in you, then it really doesn't matter what people think about you or say about you or do to you. You will want to cry sometimes, but God won't look with disfavour on your tears. You will come up to time, and embrace his will, and put down your gold coronet, cheerfully enough, at the feet of that Saviour who was crowned with thorns.

CHAPTER 22

Man the Misfit

Not that I count these present sufferings as the measure of that glory which is to be revealed in us. If creation is full of expectancy, that is because it is waiting for the sons of God to be made known. Created nature has been condemned to frustration: not for some deliberate fault of its own, but for the sake of him who so condemned it, with a hope to look forward to: namely, that nature in its turn will be set free from the tyranny of corruption, to share in the glorious freedom of God's sons. The whole of nature, as we know, groans in a common travail all the while. And not only do we see that, but we ourselves do the same; we ourselves, although we have already begun to reap our spiritual harvest, groan in our hearts, waiting for that adoption which is the ransoming of our bodies from their slavery. (ROM. 8:18–23)

SOMETHING TELLS ME THAT ALL THIS DOESN'T MEAN VERY much more to you than if I'd read it out in the original Greek. And yet it's rather a jolly epistle really, only it wants a bit of translating, and it wants a bit of commenting on.

It is all about the Fall of Man, which is not mentioned. St. Paul has alluded, quite incidentally, to the fact that Christians must expect to endure sufferings here, if they are to enjoy the glory of heaven later on. And then he says, "Of course, you must understand that the glories of heaven are quite out of proportion to our sufferings here." By which I think he means that our sufferings here are really nothing to write home about, if you consider what this world is and what is going to happen to it, a fallen world destined to go up in smoke. I don't think you can say that at the time when St. Paul wrote this epistle the Christians were actually being persecuted; it was only some years later that the Roman emperors started persecuting. They may have got rather a rough house sometimes from their Jewish neighbours, or from their Gentile neighbours who regarded them as a sect of Jews. But in any case, I don't suppose they lived very comfortable lives, those Roman Christians. Many of them must have been slaves, and slaves, as we have seen, weren't always treated very well. You remember the story I told you about the old Roman who used to have a slave thrown into the pond as a treat for his fish. People don't do precisely that kind of thing nowadays—at least, I've never heard of it, but they are doing, in these times, a great many cruel things, and the total of suffering that is going on, if you read about it and then sit down to think it over, makes you feel quite sick. What St. Paul would tell us, I think, is that all this suffering is beastly, to be sure; but there is nothing surprising about it, nothing unexpected about it. It all fits in, you see, with the conditions of our life here, because we live in a fallen world.

And then he falls into that set of ruminations which forms the passage I have quoted. "If creation is full of expectancy, that is because it is waiting for the sons of God to be made known." For St.

Paul, heaven is always just round the corner; and he is so eager to get there that he reads his own feelings into the world around him, pictures nature itself as craning its neck in expectation, longing for the Last Judgement. You probably know that sort of feeling—how sometimes, when you are particularly down in the mouth, nature seems to chime in with your mood; fog or drizzling rain seems a companionable thing, and you fancy that if you met nature you would say, "Shake hands, old chap, that's exactly how I'm feeling myself." Well, St. Paul is in just the opposite mood, the mood of going home for the holidays; and he imagines the whole of nature sharing *that* mood; everything seems to shout, "It can't be long now." If you had drawn his attention, for example, to the way the sun burnt up the hillsides in summer, making the grass wither and the blossoms drop off, he would have said, "Splendid, isn't it? All getting ready for the last day, when the elements will be resolved in burning heat."

Then he goes on, "Created nature has been condemned to frustration; not for some deliberate fault of its own, but for the sake of him who so condemned it, with a hope to look forward to." Frustration—I think that's the word we want. You see, when somebody talks about vanity, all it suggests to you is looking in the looking-glass and thinking what a charming effect it has. And when we read about nature being made subject to vanity, it just doesn't mean anything, does it? But frustration, that's different. Continual effort continually defeated—that's frustration. And that, you see, is exactly what nature is. Every spring, nature puts out new life, all green and splendid, as if she was saying to herself, "At last I think I've got the better of Death! He'll find his job cut out for him, dealing with

RONALD KNOX

all those nettles! And when we cut down the nettles, they do come up again with surprising rapidity. But it's all wasted, you see; autumn comes along, and all the finery dies away, this year exactly as it did last year. It's all a long struggle between life and death; and life never wins, yet never knows when it's beaten. That is frustration, and it is characteristic of the world as we know it. "All the rivers run into the sea," the Wise Man says, "and yet the sea doth not overflow; unto the place from whence the rivers came, they return, to flow again." Perpetual process which never seems to lead anywhere, perpetual effort always baulked of its aim—that's the world, as we know it.

What makes it like that? What's the meaning of it all? Why, simply that we live in a fallen world. When Adam fell, the consequences of his sin didn't only come on him, or on us, his descendants. The world, which had been created as a Paradise for man in his innocency, now became a place in which man had to sweat and suffer. Now, don't tell me that people have dug up prehistoric skeletons and things which show that the world was a very unpleasant place, full of dinosaurs and things, long before man appeared. If so, it only means that the world outside Paradise was a world already made for fallen man, because God already knew that man would fall. When man fell, he was driven out of Paradise, a sensible kind of place in which there was no death and no suffering, and found himself an exile in this world of striving and frustration, in which he has been living ever since.

And it wasn't nature's fault, St. Paul points out, that nature was condemned to this sentence of frustration. It was Adam's fault; this singularly imperfect world was made for us singularly imperfect

The Gospel in Slow Motion

human beings to live in. That's what St. Paul means when he says, "not for some deliberate fault of its own, but for the sake of him who so condemned it"—it was Adam (or rather, if you will excuse a certain prejudice on behalf of my own sex, it was Eve) who was responsible for the whole thing. And St. Paul adds, "with a hope to look forward to." From the very first, when Adam and Eve fell, God resolved to undo that tragedy through the coming of our Blessed Lord, and the obedience of our Blessed Lady; prepared, even then, a heavenly paradise for us, which was to be something far better than the earthly paradise we had lost. That is the hope by which man has lived ever since. And St. Paul, looking round with a mystic's eye at dumb nature around him, pictures dumb nature itself as living in that same hope, the hope of new heavens and a new earth, to replace the old.

Does that mean that animals go to heaven? Many kind people keep the fourth Sunday after Pentecost, which has this epistle, as Animal Sunday, and like to think that the brute creation will somehow share in the glories of that new heaven and new earth which we look forward to. And at first sight St. Paul seems to be saying something of the kind, for he goes on, "The hope, namely, that nature in its turn will be set free from the bondage of corruption, to share in the glorious freedom of God's sons." But when you come to look into the thing, it doesn't really work out like that. Because St. Paul is not talking about animal nature; he is talking about the whole of creation; about the lettuces in the kitchen garden and the crater of Mount Vesuvius. So really, today isn't Animal Sunday, it's Thing Sunday. And even if we could believe that the lettuces in the kitchen garden and the crater of Mount Vesuvius will somehow turn up in heaven, it's absurd to suppose that the lettuces in the kitchen garden and the crater of Mount Vesuvius are actually, in cold fact, looking forward to that pleasant future. So I'm afraid there is no reason for thinking that your rabbits are looking forward to going to heaven either. No, St. Paul was talking like a mystic; and I have no doubt that if he had been making a speech in salvage week, St. Paul would have pointed to an empty sardine tin and said, "That tin is looking forward with eager expectation to becoming a tank." He is, as I was telling you just now, simply reading his own feelings into the world around him, imagining that stocks and stones and trees must be sharing in that mood of expectancy which makes him look forward so eagerly to the glory which awaits us in heaven.

All creation, he says, continuing his mystic vision, groans as if in agony. It's all a misfit, and it squeaks as a drawer squeaks in a chest-of-drawers when it doesn't fit quite properly. There are animals which can't keep alive without killing other animals; there are volcanoes with lava inside them which overflows and makes a mess of the whole countryside; there are earthquakes and tornadoes and all sorts of uncomfortable things; it's all dreadfully untidy. And into this misfit world man fits, because man is himself a misfit. "We ourselves, although we have already begun to reap our spiritual harvest"—although, that is, we have eternal life already abiding in us through our baptism—"we ourselves groan in our hearts, waiting for that adoption which is the ransoming of our bodies from slavery." We look forward to heaven not merely as a place in which our souls will be happy, but as a place in which our bodies, mysteriously restored to us, will share those conditions of happiness. Man, yes, if you like, man is a misfit, in this imperfect

The Gospel in Slow Motion

world which is all the world we know at present. Man so infinitely great, whose thought can read the secrets of nature, can sweep the heavens in their immensity, and look beyond them in thought, as he sees in them the hand of the God who made them; man so infinitely great, harnessing the forces of nature and taming the beasts to his will; man with all his splendid works of art, his exuberant fancy, his aspiration towards holiness, his capacity for receiving God. And man, at the same time, so infinitely little. Man, always making resolutions which he doesn't keep, always being blinded by prejudices and aversions which he can't account for; man looking back on his own conduct and knowing himself mean, and selfish, and degraded; there is no littleness like his. All you can say of him, then, is that he, too, is a misfit. He gets bored, for example—the dumb animals don't get bored. When a dog yawns, it's only digesting its food. But man must be always amusing himself, distracting himself; he can't bear to be left alone with his own thoughts. Why's that? Because he is a misfit; he was born for a nobler world than this transitory world, and he lives here in exile.

That's something, then, of what St. Paul means by this epistle. And it's something worth remembering and worth getting into our heads in days like these, when the whole world seems to be turned upside down and you can never guess what unpleasant piece of news will meet your eye when you open the morning paper. St. Paul would tell us that all the sufferings people are having to undergo, all the sufferings you and I may have to undergo, before the thing is finished, aren't really so very extraordinary; it's just the world, our fallen world, being true to form. Man is meant to live, not in enjoyment of this world, but in hope of the next. All his efforts to settle down and make himself comfortable here defeat their own ends; all the civilization he is so proud of only results in horrible bloodthirsty affairs like the present war, which do their best to turn us all into savages. You can't ever really feel at home in this world until you realize that you're an exile. You can't ever really make the best of this world until you begin to understand that it's only an out-of-date model which has got to be scrapped. That is how the Saints have lived; that is how the Saints have managed to alter the course of the world's history—by not minding much whether the course of the world's history was changed or not. St. Paul, for example, whose preaching changed the face of Europe; and all the time he was saying to himself, "Heaven! The adoption of the sons of God! It can't be far off now; thank goodness, it can't be far off now! The creaking machinery of this imperfect creation must surely run down at last."

CHAPTER 23

The Report

Be on your guard, against false prophets, men who come to you in sheep's clothing, but are ravenous wolves within. You will know them by the fruit they yield. Can grapes be plucked from briers, or figs from thistles? So, indeed, any sound tree will bear good fruit, while any tree that is withered will bear fruit that is worthless; that worthless fruit should come from a sound tree, or good fruit from a withered tree, is impossible. Any tree which does not bear good fruit is cut down, and thrown into the fire. I say therefore, it is by their fruit that you will know them. The kingdom of heaven will not give entrance to every man who calls me Master, Master; only to the man that does the will of my Father who is in heaven. (MATT. 7:15–21)

I DON'T KNOW HOW TO BE SUFFICIENTLY GRATEFUL FOR the coincidence which makes this particular Sunday, with its gospel about trees and their fruit, the last Sunday of term. I suppose it must happen fairly often, but you will see for yourselves what I mean, in a moment. Our Lord is talking, directly, about false prophets. He foresees that there will be, from the first, sham Christians who will try to exploit the Christian message for what they can make out of it; you come across a good many references to such people in the writings of St. Paul. And the principle which he lays down is a very simple one. You will know them by their fruits; that is, by their actions. The false prophet can practice his part well enough to pass muster at first meeting, and of course he starts out by being on his good behaviour, and acting the Christian as much as he can; but he can't keep it up, he can't stay the course; before long he will give himself away. Well, what our Lord is thinking of immediately is the behaviour of people who are conscious frauds, who only pretend to be Christians for what they can get out of it. But the principle he lays down can be extended very much wider than that. All of us, in the long run, will be known by our fruits; there is no other safe test of what we are worth, mentally or spiritually, but to judge by results.

What are we worth, mentally? All through the term we have been learning lessons at the rate of several hours a day. And it wasn't very difficult for us, while the lessons were in progress, to put on an air of pleased attention, and to ask one or two intelligent questions, by way of making the mistress think we were taking far more interest in the subject under discussion than we actually were. Now and again of course there was written work, and it was rather harder to get away with that; but methods are known to most people at school by which you can cover up your tracks fairly successfully, making it appear that one or two errors which appear in what you have written were due to inadvertence, or even perhaps to the mistress not having read your writing quite accurately. Well, so it goes on; there are one or two crises in the course of the term which have to be tided over, but you can do that with a certain amount

The Gospel in Slow Motion

of tact and blandishment; and altogether it's surprising what a lot of pleasant day-dreaming you can get through, perhaps even some quite irrelevant reading on your own account, in the course of the term, and your mistress none the wiser. Then, at the end of term, the exams come, and the tree is known by its fruits.

With the end-of-term examinations come the end-of-term reports; and here again, though from a slightly different angle, we get this uncomfortable feeling of being judged by results. All through the term, such letters as we have written home have always contained a slight element of propaganda; it could hardly be otherwise. The picture of school-life which those letters painted for the benefit of our parents or guardians was, ever so slightly, a fancy picture; we dwelt more on the nice things that were said about us than on the black marks we got from those in authority; we did everything we could to spare our parents from the discomfort of feeling any anxiety about how we were getting on, except for an occasional reference, perhaps, to financial difficulties. For a dozen weeks we have been in the fortunate position of being able to supply all the information unchecked. And now the reports have got to come, and the term will be known by its fruits.

Of course, there is one point of view which you probably don't realize, from which school-masters and schoolmistresses are permanently at a disadvantage. When they send in the reports at the end of term, they are really sending in a report on themselves, and on the school, rather than on you. Because what your fathers and mothers want to know is how you are getting on at school; and if it is clear that you aren't getting on well, they are apt to suppose that it's the school's fault, not yours. If you come out bottom of the class, they complain that you must have been very badly taught, and if you come out top of the class, they complain that the other girls at Aldenham must be very stupid. I remember once when I was teaching at Shrewsbury making my class write a report on me, which they did; but I couldn't send it round to the parents, of course, which was what I should have liked to do. But that is by the way; my point is that your school report when it reaches your parents is really a report on your school; it helps them to make up their minds whether being at Aldenham is doing you any good or not. It is the fruits of Aldenham, not the fruits of you, that are coming under the market-inspector's survey.

And now suppose that your term's report gets lost in the post. Some of you, perhaps, would be inclined to welcome that as a kind of providence. But, you see, it wouldn't really do you any good. You are your own school report. St. Paul tells the Corinthians that they are his letter, written not with pen and ink but with human materials. So I am telling you that you are your own school report; the way you behave when you get home to your parents or guardians lets them know what they are to think of Aldenham, and the teaching at Aldenham, and the nuns at Aldenham. When you talk with your mouth full, they think, "How extraordinary that the nuns shouldn't have sufficient influence over their pupils to prevent them talking with their mouths full!" When you contradict your elders, they sigh and say to one another, "That's the worst of a school run by religious; they don't cure them of uppishness!" When you show riotous appreciation of low-class jokes or bad music or something of that kind, your parents say, "What a vulgar set of girls they must be at Aldenham; I wonder if we ought to allow our Priscilla to associate

The Gospel in Slow Motion

with them." Everything you do or say may be used—I don't mean it necessarily will be used, but it may be used—as evidence against the school your parents have sent you to; they are judging the tree by you, its fruits.

I've been using rather frivolous and unimportant illustrations to show you what I mean; I did that on purpose, to make you listen better. But of course all that I've been saying applies equally in other connections. Your parents want to know how you are getting on at Aldenham, and what effect it is having on your character; and they have to judge that by the fruits—by your behaviour in the holidays.

Of course, I'm a convert, and like all converts I am apt to think, "How wonderful it must be to get a Catholic education!" Some of your parents are like that; and I think they must sometimes be a little surprised that this wonderful Catholic education sits so lightly on you when you get home. Some of your parents are non-Catholics, and *they* must be a little surprised, too, and perhaps not always altogether edified. I mean, you'd have thought, wouldn't you, that a girl who had got into the habit of going to Mass and Communion most days of the week, all through the term, would have wanted to go to Mass and Communion some days in the week during the holidays, not wanting to have a lie in bed every week-day. And some of you mean to do that, except, let's hope, on the feast of our Lady's Assumption. That is the fifteenth of August, in case you have forgotten about it, and it's a holiday of obligation. Again, you'd have thought that a girl who'd been accustomed to living with a lot of other girls under the shadow and in the atmosphere of a religious community would be able to spend a few weeks at home without quarrelling with her brothers and sisters, without being violently selfish about her pleasures and amusements, that she would have been willing to give up some of her time, some of her leisure, to other people; but does she? In those ways and in lots of other ways the tree is being judged by its fruit; Aldenham is being judged by your behaviour when you are away from Aldenham; and what sort of report of it does your behaviour give?

And I need hardly say the thing goes much further than that. You are going home for the holidays into a small world which consists of your parents and relations and a few family friends; nobody else will have the opportunity of knowing what kind of person you are. But this business of going home for the holidays is only a sort of dress rehearsal for the moment when you leave school altogether. Some of you have arrived at that moment, all of you will be reaching it sooner or later. And then you will go into a larger world, in which what you do and what you say will be noticed by other people, because of what you are. I don't say they will know exactly what school you went to; but they will know that you were brought up as a Catholic, with a great deal of trouble spent over you by a Church which takes a great deal of trouble about education. And they will estimate, from what they see of you, what that educational process is worth; some of them will be inclined to estimate from what they see of you whether that religion is true or not. "Nor knowest thou what argument thy life to thy neighbour's creed hath lent"; the tree is being judged by its fruits, here too.

I've no doubt that you have an objection to raise, if not to what I've been saying, at least to the way in which I've been putting it. You will tell me that it all sounds to you inexpressibly dreary, this idea of trying to edify your neighbour by behaving in a particular way for his benefit. "Am I to be always watching my step," you ask, "always wondering exactly what impression I am making on people around me? Am I never to be natural, always to look upon myself as a kind of sandwich-man, advertising Christianity in general and my own school in particular?" I can quite understand your feeling like that about it; but, if you will look a little more closely at what our Lord says in this passage, you will see he doesn't mean we are to be *consciously* edifying other people the whole time; rather the contrary.

You see, it's the false prophets who have to watch their step, if they want to be taken for Christians; ask themselves the whole time, "Now, let's see, what will be the effect of saying this? What impression shall I make by doing this?" Because, you see, Christian habits of life are not natural to them. The point of a Christian is that he or she is the kind of person from whom Christian conduct proceeds naturally, by the very law of their being, like fruit from a fruit tree. An apple tree or a plum tree doesn't have to sit down and think every autumn, "Now, let's see, what's it to be this year? Shall we say pears? Or how about gooseberries?" Of course it doesn't; the kind of fruit which it bears is determined by its own nature. And so it is with Christians, with real Christians. Their goodness, their kindness, their charity, their mortifications, aren't the results of laborious calculation; they behave like that because it comes natural to them to behave like that.

So, you see, this Christian education we've been talking of doesn't consist of acquiring a whole lot of different virtues and sticking them onto oneself like postage-stamps. The fruits by which it is known aren't a continual *tour de force*, a continual striving after effect, all through the holidays, and later all through life. They are the behaviour which comes natural to a person who loves Jesus Christ. And what you have to do now, at school, in order to bear the fruit of Christian living in your conduct later on, is to open your heart more and more to our Blessed Lord, give him a better welcome when he comes to you in your Communions, think of him at odd times during the day and offer yourself to him when you lie down to sleep, so that you may love him more and become more like him. Then, without any thought on your part, without any effort on your part, people will be able to see in you, and, what's, much more important, God will be able to see in you, the true fruits which a Catholic education ought to give.

CLUNY MEDIA

Designed by Fiona Cecile Clarke, the CLUNY MEDIA *logo depicts a monk at work in the scriptorium, with a cat sitting at his feet.*

The monk represents our mission to emulate the invaluable contributions of the monks of Cluny in preserving the libraries of the West, our strivings to know and love the truth.

The cat at the monk's feet is Pangur Bán, from the eponymous Irish poem of the 9th century. The anonymous poet compares his scholarly pursuit of truth with the cat's happy hunting of mice. The depiction of Pangur Bán is an homage to the work of the monks of Irish monasteries and a sign of the joy we at Cluny take in our trade.

"Messe ocus Pangur Bán,
cechtar nathar fria saindan:
bíth a menmasam fri seilgg,
mu memna céin im saincheirdd."

Made in the USA
Middletown, DE
13 March 2025